KU-392-256

Controversies in Sociology
edited by
Professor T. B. Bottomore and Dr M. J. Mulkay

2

Understanding
Social Life

in the same series

Social Theory and Political Practice
by Brian Fay

Understanding Social Life

The Method called *Verstehen*

by

WILLIAM OUTHWAITE

Lecturer in Sociology, University of Sussex

London
George Allen & Unwin Ltd
Ruskin House   Museum Street

First Published in 1975

This book is copyright under the Berne Convention. All
rights are reserved. Apart from any fair dealing for the
purpose of private study, research, criticism or review, as
permitted under the Copyright Act, 1956, no part of this
publication may be reproduced, stored in a retrieval
system, or transmitted, in any form or by any means,
electronic, electrical, chemical, mechanical, optical,
photocopying, recording or otherwise, without the prior
permission of the copyright owner. Enquiries should be
addressed to the publishers.

© George Allen & Unwin Ltd. 1975

ISBN 0 04 300050 9 *Hardback*
0 04 300051 7 *Paperback*

Printed in Great Britain
in 10 on 11 pt. Times Roman type
by Clarke, Doble & Brendon Ltd, Plymouth

D 4890/4.

GLASGOW
UNIVERSITY
LIBRARY

Preface

The issues with which this book is concerned have received little systematic discussion in the English-speaking world. Even the word *Verstehen* has no really satisfactory English equivalent. 'Understanding' is rather too broad; 'interpretative method' (the term preferred by Karl Mannheim) is less ambiguous but clumsy. I have therefore used the German word in its various forms (e.g. the adjective *verstehende*) throughout the book, sometimes translating it as 'interpretative understanding' (or just 'understanding' where the sense seems sufficiently clear).

The concept of *Verstehen* is most commonly encountered in discussions of the work of Max Weber and in works on the philosophy of social science. There is, however, so far as I know, no historical account in English of the development of the concept and the way it was used by writers in various disciplines—theologians, classical philologists, historians and philosophers of history, and finally psychologists and sociologists. H. P. Rickman's *Understanding and the Human Studies* raises some of the philosophical issues involved, but in only a very general way. Modern analytic philosophers in the Anglo-Saxon world are showing an increased interest in these questions: Peter Winch's *The Idea of a Social Science* is an extremely bold restatement of a *verstehende* position in philosophical terms derived from the later work of Ludwig Wittgenstein. G. H. von Wright, in his *Explanation and Understanding*, discusses some of the questions which arise in the essentially German tradition with which I shall largely be concerned here. Karl-Otto Apel, in his *Analytic Philosophy of Language and the Geisteswissenschaften* argues that analytic philosophy is moving closer to the central concerns of this 'human sciences' tradition.

Of the pioneers of a *verstehende* approach to historical and social reality, only Max Weber has been at all fully translated, and much even of his work is still not available in English (including some important methodological essays). Selections from Dilthey's work are available in H. A. Hodges's *Wilhelm Dilthey: An Introduction*. Rickman has also published a selection which includes a useful glossary of Dilthey's central concepts, entitled *Meaning in History*. A crucial essay, 'The Understanding of the other Persons and Their Life-Expressions' is printed in *Theories of History*, edited by Patrick Gardiner. Heinrich Rickert's *Naturwissenschaft und Kulturwissenschaft*, originally published in 1899, is available under the title *Science and History*, but his major work, *Die Grenzen der naturwissenschaftlichen Begriffsbildung*, seems unlikely (in view of its extreme length) ever to be translated. There is, as far as I know, no translation of Simmel's essay on historical understanding, published in 1918 (*Vom Wesen des historischen Verstehens*) nor of his *Probleme der Geschichtsphilosophie*.

I am extremely grateful to Tom Bottomore for his encouragement and criticism over the past two years. I should also like to thank Michael Mulkay, Zev Barbu, Roy Bhaskar, Ivor Hunt, Larry Ray, Helen Roberts, Gillian Rose and especially Michèle Barrett. My parents encouraged me to spend some time learning German, but for which I should not have been able to read much of the material discussed in this book.

For my fairly extensive quotations from Karl Mannheim's *Essays on The Sociology of Knowledge,* I must thank Messrs Routledge & Kegan Paul Ltd.

Contents

1

Introduction

The concept of interpretative understanding or *Verstehen* was at the centre of the methodological debates carried on by German-speaking historians and sociologists in the late nineteenth and early twentieth centuries. The idea of an interpretative *verstehende* method, which could be set against the method of causal explanation, encapsulated a characteristically German hostility to the 'positivistic' social thought of France and England, represented by men like Auguste Comte and J. S. Mill.[1]

The concept of 'understanding', then, is the nub of a long-standing theoretical controversy about the sort of method which is appropriate to a social science. On the one hand there are those who argue that social science should follow as closely as possible the well-tried methods of the natural sciences and look for general laws in social life. This was the view expressed by Comte, Mill and (in a rather different way) Karl Marx, who wrote, 'Natural science will one day incorporate the science of man, just as the science of man will incorporate natural science; there will be a *single* science.'[2] But where Marx envisaged a rapprochement of the two sorts of science, the logical positivists of the Vienna Circle[3] meant by 'unified science'

[1] Leszek Kolakowski's *Positivist Philosophy* (Harmondsworth, Penguin, 1972) is a good general account of positivism in its many different forms.

[2] Karl Marx: 1844 mss. In T. B. Bottomore and M. Rubel (eds), *Karl Marx: Selected Writings in Sociology and Social Philosophy* (Harmondsworth, Penguin, 1963), p. 85. Marx's position is discussed in Chapter 5.

[3] On the Vienna Circle and the 'unified science' movement which grew out of it, see L. Kolakowski, op. cit., and O. Neurath, 'Unified Science as Encyclopedic Integration', *International Encyclopedia of Unified Science*, Vol. 1, No. 1 (University of Chicago Press, 1938).

Neurath's view of sociology is clearly expressed in an essay 'Empirical Socio-

(*Einheitswissenschaft*) that all other sciences should be modelled as closely as possible on physics.[4]

On the other hand are those who claim that the social sciences differ from the natural sciences either in the character of their subject matter or in their methods or both. The sociologist's or historian's understanding of the people he studied was variously conceived as following unproblematically from what they had in common as human beings, or as involving some imaginative act such as the 'reliving' of their experiences; it functioned as either an alternative or, in a less extreme formulation, a necessary preliminary or complement to the identification of causal regularities in their behaviour. This tradition is associated with the names of Dilthey, Rickert, Simmel and Max Weber in Germany; there are certain parallels in the work of Croce and Gentile in Italy and Collingwood in England.[5]

More recently, Talcott Parsons's *Structure of Social Action*[6] was close to this tradition, but in his later work the elements of *Verstehen* were obliterated by his recourse to functionalism and system theory. Although few post-war social scientists would have defended in its extreme form the logical positivist thesis of the unity of science, a certain positivist consensus prevailed in which controversies over *Verstehen* were identified with the philosophy of history and the prehistory of social science. They were not wholly forgotten, since sociologists in particular take a keen, if selective, interest in the 'founding fathers' of their subject, and any discussion of Weber's sociology inevitably raised these questions. As far as current practice went, however, Theodore Abel's thoroughly purged version of the claims of *Verstehen* was widely regarded as the last word on the subject.[7]

If there was a positivist consensus in the post-war years it has certainly broken down now. The rebirth of Anglo-Saxon analytic philosophy presided over by Wittgenstein led to very different

logy' published in 1931 and reprinted in O. Neurath, *Empiricism and Sociology* (Dordrecht, Reidel, 1973).

[4] This programme can be formulated in several different ways. See A. Ryan (ed.), *The Philosophy of Social Explanation* (OUP, 1973), Introduction.

[5] Carlo Antoni, *From History to Sociology* (London, Merlin Press, 1959), discussed Dilthey, Weber and others from a Crocean position. See also R. G. Collingwood, *The Idea of History* (OUP, 1946).

[6] T. Parsons, *The Structure of Social Action* (Glencoe, Free Press, 1949).

[7] Theodore Abel, 'The Operation Called *Verstehen*', *American Journal of Sociology*, Vol. 54 (1948).

accounts of language, science and human behaviour from those advanced earlier by the logical positivists.[8] In sociology, too, scepticism about functionalism and system theory combined with impatience, in a more ideologically conscious period, with small-scale empirical research, to produce an atmosphere of self-doubt. At the same time, sociological movements claiming allegiance to phenomenology once again expressed the claims of a *verstehende* sociology in an extremely strident form. In tracing the history of the concept of 'understanding' and its adoption by influential social theorists, I shall try to show that the original controversies continue to haunt modern social thought.

Despite the mystique with which the concept of *Verstehen* has been invested, there seems no reason to suppose that historical or socio-logical understanding is essentially different from everyday under-standing. As Georg Simmel put it, 'The relation of one mind to another which we call understanding is a basic fact of human life. Insight into specifically historical understanding rests on insight into understanding in general.'[9] This is, of course, merely to say that everyday understanding is a highly complex activity. The essential distinction between 'psychological' (or sometimes, 'genetic') under-standing and the 'hermeneutic' understanding of meaning can be illustrated, at least in outline, in ordinary language.

The things which we conventionally claim to understand about other people can be conveniently broken down into four main categories:

1. *'physical'* facts about them: why they limp, why their noses are broken (a recent fight) or red (drink, sunburn, etc.). In the sense of the word which is relevant here, these phenomena are only 'under-stood' when they are seen as *signs* of something non-physical (a past event or a mental state);
2. their *states of mind*; these may be short-term (a fit of anger) or long-term (a vindictive disposition);[10]
3. *what* they are doing (and what they *mean* by it). This very broad category includes for example, (*a*) the mere identification of actions

[8] See K.-O. Apel, *Analytic Philosophy of Language and the Geisteswissenschaften* (Dordrecht, Reidel, 1967); and G. H. von Wright, *Explanation and Understanding* (London, Routledge, 1971).
[9] G. Simmel, '*Vom Wesen des historischen Verstehens*' in *Brücke und Tür* (Stuttgart, Koehler, 1957).
[10] There is no need at this level to raise the question whether propositions about mental states can or should be reduced to statements about dispositions to overt behaviour.

(for example, as we approach a figure in the distance, we see that he is chopping wood); (*b*) at the same elementary level, *what people say*; (*c*) more complex judgements about the *real* import of what they are doing, or what they *really* mean by what they say;
4. *why* people do things, what 'motivates' them.

The distinction which I am trying to establish is between points 3 and 4 above. It might be argued that this distinction is impossible to make, since to understand the meaning of human actions either is identical with, or presupposes a grasp of the motives or at least the intentions which underlie those actions. Thus, Runciman suggests that it may be just a verbal question at which point the identification of an action as an action of a certain type shades into what Max Weber would call the (explanatory) understanding of that action in terms of motives.[11] But I would suggest that while *some* decisions about how to describe an action may require a decision about the motives which underlie it, this is not always the case. The answer seems to lie in Weber's concept of the ideal type as it arises in his discussion of the term 'action' at the beginning of *Economy and Society*. If one follows Weber in defining action by the presence in the actor's mind of an 'intended meaning' (*gemeinter Sinn*), this meaning, he writes, may *either* be empirically present in the specific case under investigation *or* be merely attributed to the actor in an ideal-typical way.[12] This, I suggest, is what we usually do when we are concerned to find out 'what is going on' in a social situation. To identify an observed piece of behaviour as a conventional action of a certain sort is to rule out some questions about motivation, or at least to shift the question of the actor's motivation to another level. Thus we understand *why* people are marching in the street if we are told that a demonstration is taking place, although at another level the question why people go on demonstrations is still an interesting one (as are the private motives of the individual participants in this particular case). Similarly, we often understand the *words* someone utters without understanding what *motivated* him to say what he said.[13] This may also work in the other direction. As Weber pointed

[11] W. G. Runciman, *A Critique of Max Weber's Philosophy of Social Science* (Cambridge University Press, 1972), p. 27.

[12] Max Weber, *Economy and Society*, trans. Reinhard Bendix and Günter Roth (New York, Bedminster, 1968), Vol. 1.

[13] Rickert gives the rather nationalistic example of a German in 1918 expressing his satisfaction at the Treaty of Versailles. (H. Rickert, *Die Grenzen der naturwissenschaftlichen Begriffsbildung* (Tübingen, Mohr, 3rd/4th edn., 1921), p. 437.

out, a soldier may try to make out the sense of an ambiguously worded order by thinking about the probable intentions of the man who issued the order.[14]

In the case of works of art and other cultural products, the distinction is, in principle at least, easier to draw. In 'psychological' understanding, works are seen as 'signs' or 'expressions' of the mental life of their creators, and the imaginative penetration or reconstruction of this mental life is the principal concern of the interpreter. In 'hermeneutic' understanding the works are grasped as autonomous objects with an inner structure of their own. With this goes the contrast between genetic explanation 'from below' and an alternative method of interpretation 'from above' which operates by situating a work of art in a broader context, seeing it, for instance, as an expression of the *Weltanschauung* of a particular class.[15]

Reference to mental states raises many complex problems which also occur in the attribution of motives. Without going into the mystique which surrounds the notion of 'empathy',[16] I think it can be said that we 'understand' people's states of mind (and make inferences about their motives and intentions) with the aid of: (*a*) visible signs, voluntary or involuntary (frowns, twitches, etc.); (*b*) explicit statements ('I am angry'); (*c*) a knowledge of the 'facts of the situation' which leads us to expect one sort of attitude or intention rather than another.

It seems that in an important sense (*c*) is prior to (*a*) and (*b*). Explicit avowals of type (*b*) are probably fairly rare in real life (especially in England). Signs are ambiguous; it is usually the context which enables one to distinguish a frown of concentration from one of annoyance. And it is worth noting that when we say we understand someone's disappointment, anger, etc., or his motives for a certain action, we mean not that we know what it is to feel these emotions or the force of certain motives (this would generally be either platitudinous or, in the case of more recherché emotions and desires, perhaps not true), but rather that we understand the 'situation' in which these emotions or intentions 'make sense'. It is

[14] Max Weber, *Gesammelte Aufsätze zur Wissenschaftslehre* (Tübingen, Mohr, 3rd edn., 1968), p. 95.

[15] See Mannheim's review of Lukács's *Theory of the Novel*, to which I refer on p. 71.

[16] See, for instance, Max Scheler, *The Nature of Sympathy* (London, Routledge, 1970).

this sort of understanding, presupposing a certain community of outlook, which I have called hermeneutic.[17]

Many descriptions of mental states are conceptually or logically related to certain types of action; they have an intentional or teleological component.[18] However, it is extremely difficult to identify explanations in terms of mental states as species of psychological (or genetic or motivational) understanding on the one hand, or hermeneutic understanding on the other. Daniel Taylor seems to place them in the latter category when he calls them a species of 'what-explanations'.[19] This seems likely to blur the issues, unless one arbitrarily restricts the term 'mental state' to those which do have this teleological reference.

The important point, I suggest, is the more general one that the identification of an action *as* an action of a certain sort *and* an appreciation of its 'deeper significance' are to be distinguished from its causal explanation in terms either of efficient *or* of final causes. I shall try to show that the claim that human actions are 'meaningful' involves more than a reference to the conscious purposes and intentions of individuals. Moreover, to discuss the 'meaning' of an action is not necessarily, I shall argue, to indulge in speculative philosophy of history; it is part of the very basic process of identifying actions which must precede any formal or informal social theory.

I shall suggest, in an argument which owes much to the work of Jürgen Habermas,[20] that the residual truth of the thesis of 'methodological dualism' is that social phenomena and, in particular, human actions are not 'given' to the investigator in the same way as natural phenomena. The social scientist must begin with data which are already partially interpreted in the ordinary language of everyday

[17] This term, derived from the Greek word for interpretation, was originally used mainly in theological discourse and, as we shall see, gradually extended to other areas of intellectual inquiry.

[18] Cf. Charles Taylor's article, 'Explaining Actions', *Inquiry* (1970). Also D. Taylor, *Explanation and Meaning* (Cambridge University Press, 1970), p. 43.

[19] P. Taylor, op. cit. p. 48.

[20] In particular, J. Habermas, *Zur Logik der Sozialwissenschaften* (Frankfurt, Suhrkamp Verlag, 2nd edn, 1970). Habermas himself for some time opposed the republication of this work, on the grounds that the processes by which one clarifies a problem for oneself should not be confused with their results (ibid. Preface). It remains, however, in my opinion, a brilliant synoptic view of the most important trends in modern social thought.

life. Moreover, social scientists cannot coherently aim to provide a natural science of human life, but rather to deepen, systematise and often qualify, by means of empirical and conceptual investigations, an 'understanding' which is already present.

2

Understanding, Interpretation
and Hermeneutics

The relation between these terms is not made clear by any of the writers discussed in the following chapters, although by examining this tradition one can get a general idea of the ways in which each term is most often used. Given this diversity and inconsistency of usage, there is little point in imposing a rigid distinction between 'understanding' (*Verstehen*) and 'interpretation' (*Deutung* or *Interpretation*).

Very roughly one can say that 'interpretation' tends to be from a particular theoretical perspective (as in 'the Marxist interpretation of history'), while 'understanding' suggests a more all-round approach. This is the view adopted by Joachim Wach in his three-volume *Sketch of the History of Hermeneutic Theory in the Nineteenth Century*.[1]

'By interpretation we understand . . . investigation and explanation from the perspective of a *given system*, within which the attempt is made to grasp what is given. When the old hermeneutic writers said *"sensus non est inferendus, sed eferendus"* [meaning must be read out of, not into the text] they were trying to distinguish understanding [*Verstehen*] from *interpretation*, not just from arbitrary exegesis. . . .

'Understanding in contrast to interpretation is characterised by the attempt, in the knowledge of [the] conditioned nature . . . [of interpretation] . . . to overcome or at least neutralise it'. [i.e. this conditionality][2]

[1] Joachim Wach, *Das Verstehen: Grundzüge einer Geschichte der hermeneutischen Theorie im neunzehnten Jahrhundert* (Tübingen, Mohr, 3 vols, 1926, 1929, 1933).
[2] ibid., Vol. II, p. 9.

The concept of understanding which is relevant here was first elaborated in a theological context. The Protestant reformers proclaimed that scripture could be directly understood, without the mediation of an ecclesiastical tradition.[3] Theology retained its dominant position in the development of the theory of understanding until the middle of the eighteenth century,[4] when philology and jurisprudence took up the theme. Philosophers, with the exception of Spinoza and, later, Herder, played little part; as Wach says in relation to Kant, 'the transcendental theory of idealism was basically not particularly concerned with questions of historical understanding'.[5]

Wach mentions in particular two classical philologists, Friedrich Ast and F. A. Wolf. Ast, whose principal works were published in 1808, saw his subject as the study of the classical world centred on the 'spirit of antiquity'; this spirit was most clearly expressed in literary works but was also reflected in the public and private life of the peoples of classical antiquity.[6] One must approach the ancient world with understanding (*verstehend erkennen*) in order to learn from it and to give a complete account of its internal structure.[7] As Wach points out, the idea of the essential unity of human nature or the human mind (the highly questionable foundation on which most hermeneutic theories rest) is already present in Ast's work in a fully developed form.[8] We would not understand either antiquity in general or individual documents and works of art 'if our spirit were not essentially at one with the spirit of antiquity, so that it can absorb into itself this spirit which is only temporally and *relatively* alien'.[9] 'All grasp and understanding not just of an alien world but even of another person is simply impossible without the original unity and a likeness of all spiritual content (*alles Geistigen*) and without the original unity of all things in the Spirit.'[10]

F. A. Wolf lived from 1759 to 1824 and was active in Halle and Berlin. Wach mentions in particular his tendency to conceive the

[3] ibid., Vol. I, p. 13. Wach mentions Dilthey's contention that hermeneutics in a strict sense was possible only after the Reformation.

[4] ibid., Vol. I, p. 15.

[5] ibid., Vol. I, p. 18.

[6] ibid., Vol. I, p. 33.

[7] ibid., Vol. I, p. 36.

[8] loc. cit.

[9] ibid., Vol. I, p. 39.

[10] ibid., Vol. I, p. 37. This quotation and the preceding one are Wach's paraphrase of Ast.

purpose of hermeneutics in psychological terms, the aim being to grasp as literally as possible the intentions of a writer or speaker, to understand his thoughts in the way he wanted them to be understood.[11]

Friedrich Schleiermacher's first *Akademierede* of 1829 discussed Ast and Wolf, emphasising the complementarity of grammatical and psychological understanding. Interpretation is an act involving the 'construction of something finite and determinate from what is infinite and indeterminate'.[12] There can be no system of inflexible rules for such an activity which requires both linguistic ability and a knowledge of human beings. Schleiermacher's main contribution was to a theological hermeneutics, which may be said to have reached its height with him,[13] but the principle for which he is famous, that one should understand an author better than he understood himself, is clearly open to more general application.

Although Dilthey ended his essay on the rise of hermeneutics[14] with Schleiermacher's death in 1860, Wach demonstrates a certain continuity through the great historian Leopold von Ranke, who died in 1886, and the philologist August Boeckh down to J. G. Droysen and Dilthey himself. Boeckh emphasised that men can understand one another without an explicit theory, just as they can think coherently without following an explicit logic; both are arts. Logic is the formal theory of philosophical cognition (*Erkennen*), and the theory of understanding is the formal theory of philology.[15] Boeckh drew up an interesting typology of interpretation according to which a work may be understood in terms of the 'objective or subjective conditions of what is communicated'. The former consists of 'grammatical interpretation' of literal meaning and, secondly, historical interpretation in relation to the objective situation (*reale Verhältnisse*). Interpretation in terms of subjective conditions may relate to the subject of the utterance alone (individual interpretation) or what he calls 'generic interpretation' in terms of the direct purpose and general direction of the work.[16]

[11] ibid., Vol. I, pp. 68f. Wolf's *Darstellung der Altertumswissenschaft nach Begriff, Umfang, Zweck und Wert* was published in 1807.

[12] ibid., Vol. 1, pp. 114f.

[13] Cf. ibid., Vol. 1, pp. 24f: 'Never before or since has the theory of hermeneutics been so universally understood, developed and presented.'

[14] W. Dilthey, *Gesammelte Schriften* (Stuttgart, Teubner, 4th edn 1964), Vol. V (*Die Entstehung der Hermeneutik*), pp. 317–38.

[15] Wach, op. cit., Vol. I, pp. 191f.

[16] ibid., Vol. I, pp. 196f.

Ranke frequently discussed historical understanding, in which he saw the principal task of the historian[17], but in a very general sense in which it means little more than letting the facts speak and learning from them, as distinct from forcing them into an *a priori* schema. Ranke, Wach argues, gave the concept of 'understanding' much of its characteristic resonance, but for the first detailed account of historical understanding, in which its relevance to the emergent social sciences becomes clear, one must turn to the philosopher of history, Johann Gustav Droysen (1838–1908).

Droysen was implacably hostile to the positivist trends which, he believed, were gaining ground in Germany. Karl-Heinz Spieler, the author of a recently published thesis on Droysen, quotes a letter of 1852: 'Crass positivism unfortunately is finding great support in the development of the German sciences themselves.'[18] He expressed his opposition to positivist historiography and the search for universal laws in history in a highly critical review, published in 1862, of H. T. Buckle's *History of Civilisation in England*.

Like most of the writers discussed here, Droysen premised his theory of understanding on the separation of *Natur* and *Geist*, nature and mind, and the fundamental unity of human nature.

'The possibility of understanding rests in our familiarity with the expressions which are present as historical materials. It depends on the fact that the nature of man [*sinnlich geistige Natur des Menschen*] expresses every inner process in a way which can be perceived by the senses, and reflects inner processes in every expression. An expression projects itself into the person who perceives it and excites the same inner process. When we hear a cry of anguish, we experience the anguish of the person who uttered it. . . .'[19]

Taken in isolation, this account may seem mechanistic to the point of absurdity. But it was not Droysen's intention to explain understanding in terms of a mechanistic psychology. He carefully distinguished the *act* of understanding from what he called the 'logical mechanism' involved.[20] Karl-Heinz Spieler suggests that he used the term 'understanding' in at least three senses which he failed to distinguish:

[17] ibid., Vol. I, pp. 93ff.
[18] K.-H. Spieler, *Droysen* (Berlin, Duncker, 1970), p. 20, n. 6.
[19] J. G. Droysen, *Grundriss der Historik* (Halle-Saale, Niemeyer, 1925), para. 9.
[20] ibid., para. 11.

1. the intuitive act of understanding. These intuitions and the hypotheses to which they give rise must prove themselves in confrontation with the historical material;[21]

2. the understanding of expressions (*Ausdrucksverstehen*). 'Expressions' for Droysen are 'all phenomena of human behaviour in which we can identify psychic content [*Seelisches*]'. And the understanding of expressions is the mental process in which we perceive psychic content in the expression, in which we understand an expression as the expression of something internal.[22] The understanding of expressions also seems, according to Droysen, to have an intuitive element which must be subjected, so far as it can be, to 'objective measures and controls';[23]

3. Droysen's third sense of 'understanding' belongs to philosophical anthropology. He sees it as man's most characteristically human capacity, 'the most basic tie between men and the basis of all moral existence'.[24]

Spieler seems right to say that Droysen neglects a further possible type of understanding, the hermeneutic understanding of the meaning of linguistic expressions. Droysen might have developed this theme in his discussions of language, but he sees language merely as an expression of internal mental activity ('*Das Sprechen ist nichts als ein Äusserlichmachen des Inneren*').[25] On the other hand, he clearly recognises the limits of a purely psychological understanding: 'If psychological interpretation were the essential task of the historian, Shakespeare would be the greatest historian.'[26] As he puts it in another paragraph: '*In den Wirklichkeiten wirken noch andere Momente, als die Persönlichkeiten.*'[27] ('It takes more than personalities to constitute real processes.')

Droysen tends to use the words 'understanding' and 'interpretation' as synonyms; in other words, he is mainly concerned with the broadly psychological process of interpretation which corresponds to his account of understanding. But he also at times discusses interpretation from a logical or methodological point of view, in which past events are 'interpreted' in terms of their context and the con-

[21] Spieler, op. cit., p. 118.
[22] ibid., p. 119.
[23] ibid., p. 129.
[24] ibid., p. 123.
[25] ibid., p. 124.
[26] J. G. Droysen, *Historik* (Munich/Berlin, Oldenbourg, 1937), pp. 173–80.
[27] Droysen, *Grundriss der Historik*, para. 41.

ditions which brought them about.[28] As Droysen put it: 'The essence of interpretation is to see in past events realities with the full range of conditions which realised them.'[29]

Droysen's work is full of brilliant insights trenchantly formulated, but it is essentially programmatic; many of his insights were given a fuller theoretical expression by Dilthey and others. In particular, Droysen established the crucial connection between the theory of understanding and the philosophy of history[30] from which the idea of a *verstehende* social science eventually grew. And in drawing this connection, he emphasised that the spontaneous understanding which exists between human beings in everyday social life must be systematised with the aid of theoretical knowledge. In a passage already mentioned, Droysen wrote:

'Of course we have an immediate and subjectively certain understanding of human affairs, of every expression and every trace of human creativity and endeavour which we can perceive and in so far as we can perceive it. But we must find a way to obtain objective measures and controls for this immediate subjective conception and thereby to establish, correct and deepen it. It seems that this alone can be the meaning of the "historical objectivity" which is so often mentioned.'[31]

This, again, is a theme which greatly preoccupied Dilthey and Max Weber.

[28] Spieler, op. cit., p. 77.
[29] Droysen, *Grundriss der Historik*, para. 37.
[30] Cf. Wach, op. cit., Vol. I, p. 27.
[31] Quoted by Spieler, op. cit., p. 129.

3

Wilhelm Dilthey

The central figure in the history of the concept of *Verstehen* is of course Wilhelm Dilthey (1833–1911). The son of a Protestant pastor in the Rhineland, he studied at the University of Berlin, returned as Professor of Philosophy in 1882, and remained there until his death. Although he was principally concerned with the philosophical foundations of the 'human sciences' (*Geisteswissenschaften*) Dilthey was also active in the fields of intellectual history and biography; he wrote extensively on the Renaissance and the Reformation, on Schleiermacher and on Hegel's early life. His history of the development of hermeneutics is particularly important since he saw in hermeneutics a necessary mediating factor between philosophy and the individual human sciences, and the latter's essential foundation.

Dilthey returned again and again to the same intractable problems of the 'foundation of the human sciences' without ever achieving a definitive expression of his views. He was greatly influenced by Droysen and Schleiermacher and also by Kant, who was the object of renewed interest as a result of the reaction against Hegelian speculative philosophy.[1] Dilthey's own position moved rather uneasily between the twin poles of British empiricism (flavoured with Comtean positivism) and post-Kantian German philosophy.

We are concerned here only with Dilthey's account of *Verstehen* and his attempt to distinguish between the natural and the human sciences, but it should be remembered that his real project was a more ambitious one: a 'critique of historical reason' which would reflect on what made possible the sciences which took the human mind as

[1] H. A. Hodges, *Wilhelm Dilthey: An Introduction* (London, Routledge, 1944), p. 6.

their *object*, and thus overcome the epistemological division between subject and object. 'The first condition of the possibility of historical science lies in the fact that I am myself a historical being, that the historical researcher also makes history.'[2]

Although Dilthey began with the aim of reconstructing the *Geisteswissenschaften* and gradually resigned himself to taking them as he found them,[3] he was concerned throughout with their logical foundations. They were distinguished from the natural sciences, he thought, by their content and not by their mode of operation (*Erkenntnisweise*).[4] 'In contrast to the natural sciences there arise *Geisteswissenschaften* because we are obliged to endow human and animal organisms with mental activity (*seelisches Geschehen*).'[5] Experience, not in the empiricist sense of *Erfahrung* but in the *lebens-philosophisch* sense of 'lived experience', *Erlebnis*, functions as a sort of transcendental principle for Dilthey.[6] The importance of the

NB

[2] W. Dilthey, *Gesammelte Schriften* (*GS*) (Leipzig and Berlin, Teubner), Vol. VII, p. 278. This is essentially an echo of the familiar idea, associated particularly with Giambattista Vico (1668–1744), that in order really to know something, it is necessary to have made it. The human mind can understand the historical (or sociocultural) world which it has produced, in a way in which only God can understand the natural world. Cf. Isaiah Berlin, 'A Note on Vico's Concept of Knowledge', G. Tagliacozzo (ed.), *Giambattista Vico. An International Symposium* (Baltimore, Johns Hopkins Press, 1969).

[3] Raymond Aron, *La Philosophie critique de l'histoire* (Paris, NRF, 1969), p. 38.

[4] Dilthey, op. cit., Vol. V, p. 253.

[5] ibid., p. 249.

[6] *Lebensphilosophie*, the 'philosophy of life', is generally thought to originate in the work of Dilthey, Nietzsche and Bergson, as a reaction against what was seen as the excessive rationalism of traditional philosophy, especially that of Kant. As Dilthey put it (*GS*, Vol. I, p. xviii): 'What flows in the veins of the knowing subject constructed by Locke, Hume and Kant is not real blood but the watered-down juice of reason as a purely cognitive activity [*als blosser Denktätig-keit*].' Dilthey's concept of the *Erlebnis* has been analysed in detail in a book by Karol Sauerland, *Diltheys Erlebnisbegriff* (Berlin, de Gruyter, 1972). The concept of *Erlebnis* was developed in early nineteenth-century literary criticism, and it was used from the beginning in an evaluative way. 'Only someone who wrote on the basis of an "experience" could create literature which would pass the test of time' (Sauerland, p. 13). Dilthey emphasised, especially in his earlier works, that creative writing 'is always the expression of the writer's *Erlebnis* and arises out of the need to give expression to that experience. He therefore always tries to approach the work by way of the writer' (ibid., p. 122).

This does not mean, however, that his interpretations are made in terms of individual psychology. Though he sees Hölderlin's poetry, for instance, as an expression of inner content (*des Inneren*), he 'does not force this content into a narrowly subjectivistic frame, but also sees the external conditions [such as the

Erlebnis seems to lie in its reflexive quality; men can be studied by natural science, but only up to the point where human conditions are experienced (*erlebt*). At this point, man becomes the object of the *Geisteswissenschaften*, which are 'all founded in lived experience, in the expressions of these experiences, and in the understanding of these expressions'.[7]

Dilthey's work can conveniently be divided into two periods: an early one in which the emphasis is individualistic and psychologistic, and a later period, under the influence of Hegel,[8] in which the concept of objective mind or spirit (*objektiver Geist*) supplants the earlier individualism. The emphasis shifts from the empathetic penetration or reconstruction of other people's mental processes to the hermeneutic interpretation of cultural products and conceptual structures. On the later view, a man understands other people and even himself, not directly but through the same complex process by which he understands arguments or works of art. 'Only his actions, his objectified (*fixiert*) life-expressions and their effect on others teach man about himself; and so he comes to know himself only via the detour of *Verstehen*.'[9]

The contrast between the individualistic and the holistic emphasis can be illustrated by two passages which anticipate the 'private language' debate which Wittgenstein initiated in modern analytic philosophy. In the *Einleitung in die Geisteswissenschaften* of 1883, Dilthey wrote: 'If we were to think of a single human being existing on earth, he would, provided that he lived long enough, develop these different mental activities . . . [Dilthey mentions philosophy, religion and art] . . . all on his own in total isolation.'[10] The later passage is very different:

'Every single human expression represents something which is common to many and therefore part of the realm of objective mind. Every word or sentence, every gesture or form of politeness, every work of art and every historical deed are only understandable because the person

French Revolution] which formed and determined Hölderlin's inner life' (ibid., p. 131). As Dilthey put it in *Das Erlebnis und die Dichtung* (Leipzig, Teubner, 3rd edn, 1910), p. 369: 'The experience (*Erlebnis*) which found expression in Hölderlin's *Hymnen* was the heroic effort of the youth of that period to realise a higher ideal of humanity in itself and in the society around it.'

[7] Dilthey, *GS*, Vol. VII, pp. 70f.

[8] Dilthey worked from 1900 to 1906 on a study of Hegel's early life.

[9] Dilthey, *GS*, Vol. VII, p. 85.

[10] ibid., Vol. I, pp. 422f.

expressing himself and the person who understands him are connected
by something they have in common; the individual always experiences,
thinks, acts, and also understands, in this common sphere.'[11]

With Dilthey's early individualism there is an emphasis on our
access to the psychological reality which visible expressions (whether
gestures or artefacts) signify. 'We call understanding that process
whereby out of sensually given expressions of mental life the latter
comes to be known.'[12] Associated with this is what amounts to a
theory of meaning: 'As in the natural sciences all lawlike knowledge
is only possible by means of what can be measured and counted in
experiments [*Erfahrungen*] and in the rules implied thereby, so in the
Geisteswissenschaften every abstract proposition is verifiable only by
means of its relation to active mental life [*seelische Lebendigkeit*] as
this is given in lived experience and understanding.'[13]

Although this approach may fairly be called psychologistic, it is
not naturalistic after the manner of Mill's psychologism. Dilthey
makes much of the distinction between analytic and descriptive
psychology, and his '*verstehende Psychologie*' is clearly a species of
the latter.[14] The emphasis here again is on the *Erlebnis*. It is not a
matter of establishing causal regularities in people's behaviour
(though as we shall see, Dilthey does toy with the idea of a positive
science of psychology) but rather of experiencing their thoughts and
emotions from the inside by 'putting oneself in their shoes' (*sich
hineinversetzen*) and reliving their experiences (*nacherleben*).

One can, I think, distinguish this idea of imagining oneself in
someone else's place from the naïve and mystical notion of empathy
which postulates some form of direct access to the contents of other
people's minds; as Wittgenstein has shown, this is not only empirically but logically impossible. Dilthey is often unjustly taxed with
this naïve view, his romantic language giving the charge some
plausibility. But even the more moderate thesis, formulated in terms
of *Nacherleben* and *Hineinversetzen*, is not without its problems. In
a passage quoted earlier, Dilthey wrote:

[11] ibid., Vol. VII, pp. 146f.
[12] ibid., Vol. V, p. 332. The concept of expression (*Ausdruck* or, in this case,
Äusserung) is normally associated with Dilthey's later work (e.g. the detailed
analysis of 'classes of life-expressions' in Vol. VII which we shall discuss later).
In this passage, however, the emphasis seems to be on psychological reality rather
than on the structure of the expression.
[13] ibid., p. 333.
[14] Cf. Hodges, op. cit., pp. 42 and 159.

'In contrast to the natural sciences, *Geisteswissenschaften* arise because we are obliged to endow animal and human organisms with mental activity. We transfer to them, on the basis of their life-expressions, an analogue of what is given to us in our own inner experience. [*Von dem, was in unserer inneren Wahrnehmung gegeben ist, übertragen wir in sie auf Grund ihrer Lebensäusserungen ein Analogon.*]'[15]

If it is taken seriously, this view entails some fairly strong claims about the identity of human nature and a rather romantic, even *lebensphilosophisch* view of the historian's role.[16]

Two problems in particular reveal the limits of the psychological understanding of other people. First, as Droysen recognised, these inferences or intuitions about others' mental states and motivations are extremely difficult to verify. Although they seem to involve categorical claims (in the sense that alternative accounts of motives can contradict one another)[17] it is not clear how one could in practice decide between two rival accounts. This problem suggests that perhaps psychological understanding should be complemented by some other procedure, the most obvious candidate being the identification of causal regularities. *Verstehen* becomes a way of generating causal *hypotheses* about human behaviour; those hypotheses can then be tested.[18]

Secondly, it is difficult to deny that 'the understanding of a single personality requires systematic knowledge for its completion'.[19] If we are trying to understand Bismarck, for example, we must know the general background, the 'facts of the situation', in order to distinguish, among other things, between the events which influenced him and those for which he was personally responsible. Propositions about the impact of Bismarck on Prussian history presuppose some

[15] Dilthey, *GS*, Vol. V, p. 249.

[16] Dilthey would probably have been prepared to accept the latter consequence; Simmel (despite his famous dictum that one need not *be* Caesar in order to understand him) embraced this view wholeheartedly: 'Experience seems to show that someone who has never loved or hated cannot understand lovers or enemies, nor a cool practical man the behaviour of an idealistic dreamer, a phlegmatic type the mental processes of a sanguine person and vice versa. Thus a personally philistine historian used to petty bourgeois life will not understand the life-expressions of Mirabeau or Napoleon, of Goethe or Nietzsche, however rich and clear they may be.' (G. Simmel, '*Vom Wesen des historischen Verstehens*', *Brücke und Tür* (Stuttgart, Koehler, 1957), pp. 61f.)

[17] Cf. Simmel, *Brücke und Tür*, pp. 75f.

[18] This, as we shall see, is the view which Weber takes, the *locus classicus* being the opening paragraphs of *Economy and Society*.

[19] Dilthey, *GS*, Vol. VII, p. 141.

sort of general awareness of the influence an individual may be expected to exert on a historical situation which confronts him.

This is clearly the point at which one looks to a systematic, generalising social science, in which *Verstehen* and *Erklären*, understanding and causal explanation, are combined. Dilthey did not believe that the use of *Verstehen* ruled out causal explanation based on comparison and generalisation; the two methods are complementary and both are employed in the '*systematic Geisteswissenschaften*', by which he means psychology, sociology, etc.[20]

Some such synthesis is attempted by most of the writers with whom we are concerned.[21] But everything depends on the *terms* on which *Verstehen* and *Erklären* are combined, and on the way in which the resulting body of knowledge is characterised. We can sketch the two positions in relation to the 'systematic knowledge' necessary to a historical understanding of Bismarck. This could be seen as an inductively based set of causal generalisations about the relations between individuals and the larger social groups in which they participate. It could also be seen, rather differently, as part of that intersubjective understanding of human beings of which our common languages are the expression *par excellence* and which is a necessary condition, not just of inductive generalisations in social science, but of all thought and experience.[22]

Dilthey provided two very different answers to this problem. We have already seen something of the first, which is frankly psychologistic. *Verstehen* and *Erklären* are combined in a descriptive psychology which underlies the other human sciences just as mathematics underlies natural science.[23] 'All human products [*Erzeugnisse*] spring from mental life [*entspringen aus dem Seelenleben*] and its relations to the outside world. Since science looks everywhere for

[20] ibid., p. 151, 'The systematic human sciences are based on the same combination of fundamental uniformities and the individualising approach developed on that foundation, and consequently on the combination of general theories and comparative methods. The general truths which they establish about social life (*das sittliche Leben*) or literature become the basis for insights into the diversities of moral ideals or literary activity.'

[21] Cf. H. Rickert, *Die Grenzen der naturwissenschaftlichen Begriffsbildung* (Tübingen, Mohr, 1921), p. 466.

[22] Peter Winch develops this view, building on Wittgenstein's central concept of the 'form of life'. P. Winch, *The Idea of a Social Science and Its Relation to Philosophy* (London, Routledge, 1958).

[23] Dilthey, *GS*, Vol. V, p. 193.

regularities [*Regelmässigkeiten*] the study of cultural [*geistige*] products must also start from the regularities in mental life.'[24]

We have already mentioned some of the problems of this psychologistic view.[25] The psychological *Grundlegung der Geisteswissenschaften* was never more than programmatic; it is not at all clear what sort of 'descriptive psychology' would actually have satisfied Dilthey, torn as he was between the rival claims of romanticism and positivism. Hodges[26] brings out this unresolved conflict: 'The very word "psychology" means something different in his writings, according as it belongs to a romantic or a positivist line of argument.'[27] The idea of a descriptive science derives, according to Hodges, from positivistic tendencies in contemporary natural science. 'But he . . . is no positivist when he actually describes the structure of mental life.'[28] E. Troeltsch had already made the point that Dilthey's psychologism was much more a matter of intuitive interpretation than of genuinely causal explanation.[29]

As Dilthey came to realise, the limits of psychological understanding are most evident in the interpretations of works of art; a full report of the creative activity of Goethe-writing-*Faust* is no substitute for the text itself. 'If we only had the writers' reports on their creative activity, and all their works were lost, how little would these reports tell us!'[30] Introspection yielded less of the content and structure of mental life than he had originally thought; this knowledge could be achieved more successfully by the interpretation, not just of cultural products or 'works' in a strict sense, but also of 'life-expressions'.[31]

---

[24] ibid., p. 372.

[25] It is, however, defended by Hodges, *Wilhelm Dilthey: An Introduction*, pp. 36–51, and has recently been argued by W. G. Runciman, *Sociology in its Place* (Cambridge University Press, 1970).

[26] H. A. Hodges, *The Philosophy of Wilhelm Dilthey* (London, Routledge, 1952), Ch. 7.

[27] ibid., p. 196.

[28] ibid., p. 210.

[29] 'It is then a genetic psychologism like that of Hume or Mill, only the psychological-causal explanation is limited and paralysed in one place after another and real understanding is basically not a matter of discursive explanation but of intuitive interpretation in terms of meaning, content and teleological movement. This new psychology and philosophy of history harbours causal-genetic and intuitively interpretative understanding in an unresolved conflict.'

[30] Dilthey, *GS*, Vol. VII, p. 321.

[31] Cf. Hodges, *The Philosophy of Wilhelm Dilthey*, pp. 213–19.

Dilthey distinguishes three classes of 'expressions of mental life' (*geistige Lebensäusserungen*):

1. Propositions (*Begriffe, Urteile, grössere Denkgebilde*). These are distinguished by their 'correspondence to logical norms'.[32] They are context-independent and are, as it were, transported from one person to another without any change in their content. 'Thus the understanding is more complete here than in the case of any other life-expression. At the same time, however, it says nothing to the person who grasps it about its relations to the rich background of mental life.'[33]

2. 'Actions form another class of life-expressions. An action does not originate in the intention to communicate, but this is given by its relationship to a purpose. An action is systematically related to the mental content which it expresses and permits probable inferences about the latter.'[34] But an action, Dilthey continues, reveals only a part of the mental life from which it sprang.

3. In the case of an *expression of experience* (*Erlebnisausdruck*), however, 'a special relation exists between it, the life from which it springs and the understanding which it generates. An expression can contain more mental content (*vom seelischen Zusammenhang*) than can be grasped by introspection'. It cannot, however, be judged true or false, but only 'authentic or inauthentic'.[35]

The 'elementary forms of understanding' (i.e. the understanding of individual linguistic or facial expressions), are underwritten, on Dilthey's account, by the concept of objective mind or spirit (*objektiver Geist*); this guarantees the possibility of intersubjective communication at the most basic level. This can be seen most clearly in the case of language. 'A sentence can be understood because of the agreement [*Gemeinsamkeit*] in a speech community about the meanings of words, inflections and syntactic organisation. . . . It is always an agreed order which establishes the relation between a life-expression and its mental content.'[36]

The 'higher' forms of understanding come into play when someone is confronted by 'an internal difficulty or a contradiction with what he knows already'.[37] Someone may misunderstand an unfamiliar reaction, or the other person may be intentionally deceiving him.

[32] Dilthey, *GS*, Vol. VII, p. 205.   [33] loc. cit.
[34] ibid., p. 206.   [35] loc. cit.
[36] ibid., p. 209.   [37] loc. cit.

Thus, for various reasons, we are led to bring other life-expressions into play or to go back to the total life-structure.[38] This may involve an inductive inference 'from individual life-expressions to the entire life-complex . . . which presupposes knowledge of mental life and its relationship to its *milieu*'.[39]

The character of this sort of knowledge is difficult to determine. Sometimes it is 'rooted in the relationship of cause and effect' (*des Erwirkten zum Wirkenden*). But much of the knowledge involved in the higher forms of understanding is, like that in the lower forms, grounded not in a causal relationship but 'in that of the expression to what is expressed' (*des Ausdrucks, zu dem was in ihm ausgedrückt ist*).[40] 'The understanding of an intellectual creation is in many cases directed only towards that structure in which the individual parts of the work emerge one after another and make up a whole.'[41] Someone watching a play can lose himself in the performance, without thinking of its construction. 'Not until the spectator realises that what he accepted as a slice of reality was in fact produced in the writer's mind self-consciously and with artistic intent does the understanding ruled by the relation of life-expressions to what is expressed in them turn into an understanding dominated by the relationship of a product to its creator.'[42]

However questionable this theory of theatrical perception, the distinction is reasonably clear; the emphasis is on the structure of the 'work' (which may be a sequence of actions, a cultural product or a mode of social organisation). In these later writings the concept of meaning (*Bedeutung*) plays an important part; Dilthey tries, not wholly successfully, to give it a structural definition. *Bedeutung*, which he calls a 'category of life', 'denotes the relation of parts of a life to the whole which is of the essence of life' (*das Verhältnis von Teilen des Lebens zum Ganzen, das im Wesen des Lebens gegründet ist*).[43] 'Just as words [*Worte*] have a meaning [*Bedeutung*], by means of which they make references, or sentences a meaning [*Sinn*] which we construct, the structure [*Zusammenhang*] of a life can be constructed out of the determinate-indeterminate meaning [*Bedeutung*] of its parts.'[44]

This theory of meaning is not satisfactorily worked out, and Dilthey also speaks of meaning as the relationship between sign and

[38] ibid., p. 210. [39] ibid., p. 211.
[40] ibid., p. 207. [41] ibid., p. 211.
[42] ibid., p. 212. [43] ibid., p. 233.
[44] loc. cit., cf. Hodges, *Philosophy of W. Dilthey*, pp. 142–7.

signified, as well as in the loose sense in which it means no more than 'importance'. But the idea that a *verstehende* approach operates by situating phenomena in a larger whole which gives them their meaning is of crucial importance for the whole tradition which we are discussing.

Dilthey argues that 'cultural organisations' or, as we would be more likely to say, 'institutions', can also be interpreted hermeneutically[45] in a way which can be contrasted with a causal-genetic explanation (in terms of their origins). And in two typically convoluted sentences, he appears to ground the possibility of a 'hermeneutic of systematic organisations' in a teleological account of their operations:

> 'Hermeneutics is possible here because there exists a relation between people and state, believers and church, scientific life and the university, according to which a common spirit, a unified form of life express themselves in a structural relationship. There exists here, then, a relationship between the parts and the whole in which the parts acquire significance [*Bedeutung*] from the whole and the whole is given its meaning [*Sinn*] by the parts. These categories of interpretation correspond to the structural system of the organisation according to which it realises a teleological purpose.'[46]

This remarkable prototype of functionalism is completed with a nod in the direction of two stock objections. First, Dilthey admits that a cultural system will always contain elements which are extraneous or inessential to what we construe as its main purpose; this is, he says, 'the basic logical problem of the science of cultural systems'.[47] And on another occasion he appears to concede that this sort of approach tends to give a much too idealised picture of history, which, he argues, involves power relations as well as ideal trends towards self-development, freedom, or whatever:

> 'Just as the self-determination of the Enlightenment brought about ministerial wars and the exploitation of subjects for the sake of the hedonistic life of the Court, as well as the drive towards the rational development of forces, so any other ordering of power relationships displays a duality [*Duplizität*] in its effects. And the meaning of history can only be sought in the meaningful relationship [*Bedeutungsverhältnis*]

---

[45] '*Auch von den Organisationen ist, wie von Einzelwerken, eine kunstmässige strenge Auslegung nötig.*' *GS*, Vol. VII, p. 265.
[46] loc. cit.
[47] loc. cit.

of all the forces which were combined in that historical conjuncture.'[48]

What then does Dilthey claim for the two methods of understanding? When he discusses psychological understanding in his later writings it is usually to emphasise its uncertainty; this was one of the reasons which led him to abandon the attempt to ground the human sciences in psychology.[49] Hermeneutic understanding is more difficult to evaluate. The first point to note is that it cannot start from scratch: 'Interpretation would be impossible if the life-expressions were totally alien. It would be unnecessary if there were nothing strange about them. It therefore lies between these two extremes.'[50] We have already seen something of the curious relation between parts and whole which is involved in the process of interpretation. 'The totality of a work must be understood through its individual propositions and their relations, and yet the full understanding of an individual component presupposes an understanding of the whole.'[51] This is the famous 'hermeneutic circle' which Dilthey rightly calls 'the central difficulty of the art of interpretation'.[52]

I cannot discuss here the various theoretical moves which attempt to differentiate this hermeneutic circle from a vicious one, since they all raise complex issues of truth and objectivity. Very briefly, Habermas, building on the work of Gadamer (whose *Wahrheit und Methode*[53] is largely concerned with just this problem), emphasised the 'involvement' of the interpreter in the same complex of experience in which the 'symbols' to be interpreted arose. 'The elements relate to the interpretative scheme neither as facts to theories nor as expressions of an object language to the interpretative expressions of a meta-language. Both, the *explicandum* and the *explicans*, belong to the same language system.'[54]

Seen in this perspective, Dilthey falls into the trap of 'objectivism', by which Habermas means a view of knowledge as the reproduction

[48] ibid., p. 187. Cf. A. Wellmer, *Critical Theory of Society* (New York, Herder & Herder, 1971), p. 47.

[49] According to Hodges, however, 'Dilthey never did finally renounce the belief in descriptive psychology as the basis of both the human studies and the theory of knowledge.' (*The Philosophy of Wilhelm Dilthey*, pp. 221f.)

[50] Dilthey, *GS*, Vol. VII, p. 225.

[51] ibid., p. 330.

[52] loc. cit.

[53] H.-G. Gadamer, *Wahrheit und Methode* (Tübingen, Mohr, 2nd edn, 1965).

[54] Jürgen Habermas, *Knowledge and Human Interests* (London, Heinemann, 1972), p. 172.

of reality which takes a single, 'scientific' frame of reference as given.[55] For although Dilthey frequently emphasises that understanding 'is always only relative and can never be completed',[56] that it 'never yields demonstrative certainty'[57] he also speaks of interpretative objectivity *conflicting* with the relevance of interpretation to practical life. The origins of the human sciences in 'life' and their permanently close relationship to it 'leads to a conflict between the purposes [*Tendenzen*] of life and their scientific aim'.[58] Scientific objectivity, he goes on (anticipating Weber's answer in 'Science as a Vocation') can be achieved only through the self-discipline of the researchers themselves: 'If there are to be human sciences in the strict sense of the word science, they [i.e. the individual researchers] must set themselves this aim ever more consciously and critically.'[59]

Despite this problem of objectivity, Dilthey had no doubt that hermeneutics is more reliable than psychology. One may misunderstand the actions and motives of historical characters, or even be deliberately misled by them, but 'the achievement [*Werk*] of a great writer or inventor, a religious genius or a true philosopher cannot but be the true expression of his mental life'.[60] The historical sceptic is right to claim that motivational connections are always doubtful 'since the individual has only a very uncertain knowledge of his own motives, and others have even less insight into them'.[61] As a result, historical scepticism 'can only be overcome when the method does not have to count on the establishment of motives . . . and psychological refinement is replaced by the understanding of cultural constructs [*das Verstehen geistiger Gebilde*]. The latter are objectified in the external world and can thus be subjected to the technique of interpretation [*kunstmässigen Verstehens*].'[62]

---

[55] ibid., pp. 69, 89f. [56] *GS*, Vol. V, p. 330.
[57] ibid., Vol. VII, p. 226. [58] ibid., p. 137.
[59] loc. cit. [60] ibid., Vol. V, p. 320.
[61] ibid., Vol. VII, p. 259.
[62] ibid., p. 260. Actions can, Dilthey believes, be understood, albeit less reliably than scientific religious, artistic or philosophical systems, once they have been completed. Dilthey seems to suggest that their motives can be reduced to a clearly defined (ideal-typical?) purpose which can be grasped within a given objective situation: 'Actions which achieve a universal significance and become historical facts are not accompanied by an awareness of motives. They do however stand in a clear relationship to the objective necessities embodied in the purposive systems and external institutions. At the same time the motives are quite irrelevant to the determination of their effects; these depend only on the imagined purpose [*Zweckvorstellungen*] and the possibilities inherent in the means which are used. . . .' (loc. cit.)

What, finally, is the relationship between hermeneutic understanding and explanation? Dilthey seems to have concluded that the two could not be clearly distinguished in many cases (despite his earlier laborious attempts to establish the difference between descriptive and explanatory science). 'Between exegesis and explanation is only a gradual divergence and not a fixed dividing-line.'[63] As Manfred Riedel puts it in his Introduction to Dilthey's *Construction of the Historical World in the Human Sciences*,[64] the methods which 'from a theoretical angle had appeared to diverge come together from the viewpoint of practical research in the human sciences'.[65] Dilthey assumed, Riedel continues, 'that the understanding of the spiritual and historical world is in itself homogeneous, from its general conception down to the methods of criticism and individual investigation'.[66] He hoped that by *describing* the methodology of the human sciences, rather than imposing on them a pre-existing logic or epistemology, he could extend the limits of logic and epistemology so as to yield a new fundamental science 'which would take over the function of justifying and regulating research in the human sciences'.[67]

Dilthey's distinction between psychological and hermeneutic understanding will recur throughout the following briefer discussions of Rickert, Simmel and Weber. Rickert is uninterested in psychological understanding but constructs an alternative to a science of causal generalisations around the concepts of 'individualisation', 'value' and 'objectivity', and his work greatly influenced Weber. Simmel makes something like the same transition from psychology to hermeneutics as did Dilthey, although even less consistently. Weber, finally, discusses only the (largely psychological) understanding of motives, but his substantive work involves both the identification of actions through the understanding of meaning (*Sinnverstehen*) and a recourse to complex conceptual structures (such as the 'spirit of capitalism') which can only be 'understood' in Dilthey's later sense of the word. The sociology of literature and knowledge of Lukács, Goldmann and the early Mannheim, also involves the latter operation. In bringing the discussion up to date, I shall argue that the

[63] ibid., Vol. V, p. 336.
[64] W. Dilthey, *Der Aufbau der geschichtlichen Welt in den Geisteswissenschaften*, edited by M. Riedel (Frankfurt, Suhrkamp, 1970).
[65] ibid., pp. 74f.
[66] ibid., p. 75.
[67] ibid., p. 67.

psychological understanding of motives can and must be integrated into social science (as Weber saw), but that the logically prior problems of the understanding of meaning are less easy to resolve.

4

Rickert, Simmel, Max Weber

Heinrich Rickert's major work, *Die Grenzen der naturwissenschaft-lichen Begriffsbildung*,[1] was first published in 1902; the 3rd/4th editions of 1921 were dedicated to the memory of Max Weber. Rickert was much more of a Kantian than Dilthey and restricted himself more to 'logical' (in the broad sense of the word) and methodological issues.[2] Unlike Dilthey, he was concerned that what he called the 'cultural sciences' (*Kulturwissenschaften*) should conform to an existing epistemology and logic. He shared Dilthey's antipositivist aim of distinguishing them from the natural sciences, but for Rickert, the important difference was one of method not content. The methods of the cultural sciences, and in particular history, are individualising and involve 'reference to values'; those of the natural sciences are generalising. This classification is ideal-typical:

'We do not mean that the one science, as it is actually practised today, operates only in a generalising manner, and the other only in an individualising way, that one is *only* concerned with non-meaningful existents [*mit sinnfreien Wirklichkeiten*] and the other only with meaningful reality.[3] We present the contrast between the historical-cultural sciences and the generalising natural sciences as the principal division of the empirical sciences of reality [*Realwissenschaften*] and emphasise that what is treated by the historical cultural sciences constitutes for the

[1] *Die Grenzen der naturwissenschaftlichen Begriffsbildung* (Tübingen, Mohr, 3rd/4th edns, 1921).
[2] Of the changes made for the second edition, he writes, 'my most important aim was to differentiate more sharply logical from psychological considerations', ibid., p. ix.
[3] ibid., p. 466.

natural scientific, generalising mode of inquiry [*Begriffsbildung*] a boundary which it can never cross.'[4]

The four-fold classification above would seem to leave open the possibility, in general terms, of a *verstehende* sociology which was both a generalising science and operated with reference to values (ignoring for the moment precisely what is meant by the latter notion). But Rickert seems to assume that a generalising science of human life, if it were successful, could only be a positive natural science.[5] If sociology tries to do this, to provide 'a natural-scientific or generalising account of social reality', there is no *logical* objection.[6] But sociology must be 'opposed most emphatically as soon as it claims to be the only science of the "historical life" of human beings or the science of history itself'.[7]

In fact, Rickert shrewdly observes, most of the best sociological works have a historical form, in which the theory functions as 'an ideal-typical orientating device' [*ein idealtypisches Orientierungs-mittel*],[8] although this material can also be used, as in Weber's *Economy and Society*, to illustrate general concepts. Later in the *Grenzen*, Rickert argues that comparative, generalising history is impossible without reference to 'cultural values' (*Kulturwerte*); even Comte, who tried to create a positive science of society, was a 'naturalist only in intention, not in practice'.

'In particular, even for Comte the connection between the different stages of history is made in evaluative terms (*wertbezogen*): he deduced the second stage as a teleologically necessary transition from the first to the last. In this respect the positivist schema of development belongs in the same logical category as the attempts made by idealist philosophers of history (e.g. Fichte or Hegel) to lay down the meaning of the whole of human history in a single formula.'[9]

Rickert means by value-reference or *Wertbeziehung*, which he rather unsatisfactorily tries to distinguish from actual evaluation (*Wertung*), the identification of something as an appropriate object

[4] ibid., p. 472.   [5] ibid., p. 196.
[6] 'However unsatisfactory the work which this science with the unsatisfactory name may sometimes produce, one cannot object from a logical point of view to a natural scientific or generalising account of social reality. . . .' (ibid., p. 196.)
[7] ibid., p. 201. Cf. W. Dilthey's early polemic, *Gesammelte Schriften* (*GS*) (Leipzig and Berlin, Teubner), Vol. I, pp. 420–3.
[8] Rickert, op. cit., p. 200. The phrase comes from Weber's '*Zwischenbetracht-ung*' at the end of the first volume of the *Religionssosiologie* (*RS I*, p. 536).
[9] Rickert, op. cit., p. 479.

of moral evaluation or 'interest'. Thus, the argument might run, one may approve or disapprove of the Russian Revolution but one can hardly be completely indifferent to its moral dimension of significance. The natural scientist also makes judgements about the significance of the phenomena he investigates, but:

> 'It is characteristic of the natural scientific approach that the objects investigated are and must be detached from all relation to values, if they are to be seen only as specific examples of general concepts. The science of history must also avoid making practical judgements on its objects and evaluating them as good or bad, but it can never lose from sight the relations of the objects to values in general, since it would then be unable to separate historically important from historically unimportant processes in empirical reality.'[10]

Max Weber followed Rickert quite closely in his theory of 'value-relevance' (*Wertbeziehung*). Neither of them, however, gave a satisfactory explanation of why the judgements which historians and sociologists obviously do make about the relative significance of the phenomena they study need necessarily be made in terms of values.[11]

Verstehen is not an important concept for Rickert, though the example of Dilthey led him to expand his discussion of it in successive editions of the *Grenzen*.[12] Psychological understanding is irrelevant to historiography, although '*Nacherleben*', the imaginative 'reliving' of the experiences of historical agents, may be employed to 'fill out' already constructed historical concepts. We have already mentioned the example of the German expressing his satisfaction at the Treaty of Versailles: 'We "understand" the non-real meaning of the other's discourse, but we are unable to "relive" the real mental processes of the man who expresses this meaning. . . . The understanding of the meaning is successful, the reliving of the mental process [*des Seelischen*] is not.'[13]

Rickert uses the concept of mental activity less widely than Dilthey, restricting it to real temporal processes in single individuals: '*Seelisch wirklich ist nur, was in einzelnen Individuen zeitlich abläuft.*'[14]

---

[10] ibid., p. 251.
[11] See W. G. Runciman, *A Critique of Max Weber's Philosophy of Social Science* (Cambridge University Press, 1972).
[12] Rickert, op. cit., p. ix.
[13] ibid., p. 437.
[14] ibid., p. 418. Dilthey's failure to distinguish *Seele* and *Geist* is not, of course, mere carelessness or a positivist suspicion of the latter concept: 'The refusal to distinguish psychological and logical elements is the result not so much of

It is not this that is 'understood', but the meaning (*irrealer Sinn*) of human behaviour or cultural phenomena.[15] There is a relatively clear statement in an early work entitled *Kulturwissenschaft und Naturwissenschaft*, translated as *Science and History*:

> 'The word "understanding" is very ambiguous, and the concept that it denotes therefore requires precise definition. The crucial question in drawing the distinction between the cultural and the natural sciences is what the *opposite* of understanding is conceived to be. We must distinguish it from perceiving and in so doing conceive the latter idea so broadly that the entire world accessible to the senses (i.e. all immediately given physical and psychical events) will be considered as the object of perception. But even then, in the interest of logical clarity we cannot rest content with the acts of the *subject* who does the understanding. On the contrary, from the methodological point of view it is the *objects* which are understood that are essential. If the entire world of phenomena directly accessible to the senses is designated as the object of perception, then only non-sensorial *meanings* or *complexes of meaning* remain as objects of understanding, if the word is to retain any precise significantion.'[16]

I shall not reproduce Rickert's polemics against the psychologism of the early Dilthey, since they are implicit in the passages already quoted. It is interesting, however, to compare Rickert's *Wertbeziehung* with Dilthey's later, hermeneutic concept of *Verstehen*. In the case of complex 'spiritual' phenomena, such as the spirit of a legal system, what is involved, according to Dilthey, is not psychological understanding but 'recourse to a conceptual construction with its own structured regularity'.[17]

The method which Rickert ascribes to history, the interpretation of phenomena in terms of their 'value' and 'meaning', is contrasted with the establishment of causal generalisations, the method of natural science. How is it related to the teleological constructions of speculative philosophy of history, the attempt to construe the whole course of history as the fulfilment of some ideal purpose? In advising

positivist prudence as of a historian's and psychologist's conviction that the spirit is simply life purified by its self-expression.' (Aron, *Philosophie critique de l'histoire* (Paris, Gallimard, 1969), p. 80).

[15] Cf. Rickert, op. cit., pp. ix, 412, 424n. 'Whatever does not in some sense have value or meaning remains incomprehensible and can therefore, even if it is anyway accessible to science, merely be described or explained in the same way as the value-less and meaning-less realities of nature.'

[16] H. Rickert, *Science and History* (New York, Van Nostrand, 1962).

[17] Dilthey, *GS*, Vol. VII, p. 85.

against the use of the word 'teleological' Rickert makes two points: 'Not only must theoretical orientation to values be sharply distinguished from valuation, but the idea of history as involving "teleological" concepts is not to be understood as implying that history is supposed to *explain* the goals consciously aimed at by the persons it deals with.'[18]

The latter point is clear enough. Teleological explanations are paradigmatically used in accounting for the action of human beings, since it is generally recognised that human beings do often act according to preformed purposes and intentions. What is at issue is whether similar explanations can be given of other sorts of entity or of the course of history in general.

Rickert would, I think, have disclaimed any such ambition. He was concerned with a method of *interpretation* with the following characteristics:

1. It does not conflict with an explanation in terms of efficient causation.[19]
2. It makes use of or incorporates such explanations.
3. It is an essential part of such explanations, serving to select the cause of a given phenomenon from the whole set of its causal antecedents.

'History, too, with its individualising method and its orientation to values, has to investigate the causal relations subsisting among the unique and individual events with which it is concerned. These causal relations do not coincide with the universal *laws* of nature, no matter how far general concepts may be required as constructive *elements* of historical concepts in order to represent *individual causal relationships*. The only thing that matters is that the methodological principle governing the selection of what is *essential* in history involves reference to values even in the inquiry into *causes*, in so far as the only causes that come into question are those which are specifically *important* for the realisation of valued ends. "Teleology" in this sense can in no way be opposed to causality.'[20]

This is an account of causal explanation as practised by historians and (much of the time) by social scientists, which deserves respect.[21]

[18] Rickert, *Science and History*, p. 93.
[19] This is, arguably, true of teleological explanations in general. Cf. Charles Taylor, *The Explanation of Human Behaviour* (London, Routledge, 1964).
[20] Rickert, *Science and History* p. 94. Cf. *Grenzen.* p. 212.
[21] It is taken up and developed by Weber, whose theory of 'causal imputation' *(kausale Zurechnung)* is clearly presented and exhaustively discussed by

Its inadequacy lies in the concept of *Wertbeziehung*, which is deficient in two respects. Firstly, there seems to be an equivocation between specifically moral relevance and 'significance' in terms of some undefined set of 'cultural values'. It is, I think, a mistake to suggest, as Louch does, that *all* explanations in history and social science are types of moral explanation.[22] Secondly, whose are the values which are invoked? Individual evaluations (*Wertungen*) can be accounted for in terms of ethical individualism, but the identification of 'value-relevance' is not meant to be a matter of individual choice: it cannot be, if it is to cover the concepts of 'meaning', significance, etc. as it is required to do. It implies, in fact, a radical historicism, as can be seen in Rickert's treatment of historical objectivity:

> 'If the historian constructs his concepts according to the values of the community to which he himself belongs, the objectivity of his account will seem to depend entirely upon the accuracy of his factual material, and the question whether this or that event of the past is important [*wesentlich*] cannot arise. . . . He is immune from the charge of arbitrariness if he relates, for example, the development of art to the aesthetic values of his culture and the development of the state to its political values. He thus creates a narrative which, so far as it avoids unhistorical value *judgements*, is valid for everyone who accepts aesthetic or political values as normative for the members of his community.'[23]

For Rickert, then, *Verstehen* is made possible by what has come to be known as 'value-consensus'.[24] Others postulate an 'objective mind' (Dilthey) or a 'linguistic community' (from Herder to Wittgenstein) or a '*Lebenswelt*' (Husserl and Schütz). Each of these answers, as we shall see, involves a form of historicism.

Georg Simmel's account of *Verstehen*, which can be found in his *Problems of the Philosophy of History*, first published in 1892,[25] and in a longish paper dating from 1918 on 'The Nature of Historical

Alexander von Schelting, *Max Webers Wissenschaftslehre* (Tübingen, Mohr, 1934).

[22] A. R. Louch, *Explanation and Human Action* (Oxford, Blackwell, 1966) draws on the same tradition in modern analytic philosophy as Winch.

[23] Rickert, *Grenzen*, p. 494. Cf. Lukács's criticisms of this position in *History and Class Consciousness* (London, Merlin, 1971), pp. 150f. Rickert continues: 'One can disagree over whether it is possible or even in any case desirable that the historian should avoid making value-judgements. This question however lies outside the scope of a logical investigation.' (p. 495).

[24] The notion that societies in some sense are 'held together' by adherence to a set of common values is a familiar theme of functionalist sociology.

[25] G. Simmel, '*Die Probleme der Geschichtsphilosophie*' (Leipzig, Duncker & Humblot, 5th edn, 1923), pp. 59–85.

Understanding'[26] need not be discussed in detail here, since it is in many ways similar to Dilthey's.[27] Like Dilthey, he makes the transition from a purely psychological[28] to a more complex notion of understanding. As Aron puts it:

'Simmel first studied understanding in a purely psychological way: what are the necessary *a prioris* for us to be able to reconstruct another person's states of consciousness? In particular, how do we manage to grasp, as a unity, the personality of another person? This last question already draws us beyond the initial formulation of the question; understanding is no longer psychological participation, but intellection.'[29]

Simmel distinguishes at an early stage between the 'objective understanding' of the meaning of an utterance and the subjective understanding of motives and intentions.[30] The 'objective understanding' of, say, Kant's philosophy must come before any genetic historical explanation: 'One must first "understand" him and the other philosophers under consideration in an objective sense [*sachlich*] . . . and only then can one "deduce him historically".'[31] We can, however, also understand someone's motives for saying what he said, and it should be emphasised that it is this type of understanding which is relevant to historical characters:

'When we perceive this motive of the utterance, we have "understood" it in a very different sense from that involved in the comprehension of its objective content; this understanding is now related not only to what is said, but to the speaker. It is this type of understanding and not the former one which arises in relation to historical personalities.'[32]

[26] Printed in the collection of his essays entitled *Brücke und Tür* (Stuttgart, Koehler, 1957).

[27] Their fundamental presuppositions were not of course the same—see Aron, op. cit., *passim*.

[28] See, for example, the first page of the *Probleme* (5th edition): 'All external events, political and social, economic and religious, legal and technical, would be neither interesting nor comprehensible to us if they did not derive from and engender psychological processes [*Seelenbewegungen*]. If history is not to be a puppet-show it must be the history of psychic processes, and all external events which it describes are nothing but the bridges between impulses and acts of will on the one hand, and on the other the emotional reactions [*Gefühlsreflexe*] which are released by these external events.'

[29] Aron, op. cit., p. 176.

[30] Weber commends him for this: *Gesammelte Aufsätze zur Wissenschaftslehre (GAW)* (Tübingen, Mohr, 1922), p. 93.

[31] Simmel, *Probleme*, p. 36n. Cf. '*Vom Wesen des historischen Verstehens*', *Brücke und Tür* (Stuttgart, Koehler, 1957), p. 77.

[32] ibid., p. 38.

One should note in passing that Simmel anticipates Weber's concept of the ideal type. The understanding of motives and emotions involves their reconstruction (*Nachbilden*) and their projection on to an imaginery ego, since they are clearly not experienced by the historian as his own.[33] What makes these processes and the connections between them 'understandable' is that they can be recognised as 'typical':

> 'Certain ideas are accompanied in our mind by the feeling that they are not only sustained by the contingent and momentary events of subjective mental life, but that they have validity as types [*typische Gültigkeit*], that one idea in itself points to its connection [*Verbundensein*] with others, irrespective of the momentary situation in the subject's mind which realises this inner relation between the ideas.'[34]

Simmel's accounts of how *Verstehen* is possible are rather unsatisfactory, involving (as above) appeals to self-evidence or, even worse, the claim that 'life' is self-explanatory: 'Life can only be understood in terms of life, and it divides itself for this purpose into levels of which one mediates the understanding of the others and their interdependence expresses the unity of life.'[35] In discussing the truth-claims of psychological and hermeneutic understanding, however, he takes, I think rightly, the opposite view to Dilthey.

The latter, it will be remembered, considered that our understanding of motives was uncertain compared to that of 'works', and that a 'work' could only be the true expression of its creator's mind. Simmel, however, emphasises that hermeneutics admits a plurality of possible and even plausible interpretations, psychological understanding only a single one.

> 'Following from what has been said before, if one, for example, understands *Faust* theoretically and aesthetically, one abstracts completely from its mental genesis; if different types of understanding [*Verständnis*] satisfy to an equal degree the requirements of logical and artistic coherence [*Zusammenhang*], uniform clarification of obscurities, and a comprehensible [*nachfühlbar*] development of the parts out of one another, they are all equally correct. If on the other hand I am to understand *Faust* historically and psychologically, that is understand the

---

[33] 'This experience [*Empfinden*] of something which I strictly speaking do not experience is the riddle of historical knowledge' (ibid., p. 41).

[34] ibid., p. 42.

[35] Simmel, '*Vom Wesen des historischen Verstehens*', *Brücke und Tür*, p. 83. On Simmel's *Lebensphilosophie*, see Rudolph Weingartner, *Experience and Culture: The Philosophy of G. Simmel* (Wesleyan University Press, 1960, 1962).

finished product [*das entstandene Gebilde*] in terms of the mental acts and developments by which it grew bit by bit in Goethe's consciousness, any such ambiguity is ruled out as a matter of principle. This process of artistic creation simply must have taken place in one particular way, which our knowledge may succeed or fail to grasp but which cannot be conceived in a number of equivalent ways. A plurality of interpretations of the genesis of *Faust*, all equally correct in the way in which a plurality of interpretations of its objective content could be correct, is a nonsense. There can, of course, be a plurality of hypotheses even about historical understanding, but in the last resort one of them is true and the others false—an alternative which does not confront an understanding in terms of objective content, where it is rather replaced by other evaluative criteria.'[36]

This does not mean, however, that psychological understanding is necessarily more certain in *practice*, since:

'it can never attain complete unambiguity, can never decide conclusively between a multiplicity of conflicting explanatory principles. The richness and flux [*Beweglichkeit*] of psychological connections is such that no 'psychological law' can decisively identify the future developments of a particular psychic constellation. Very often one development seems no less plausible than its exact opposite, depending on how we view the situation. We can understand just as well that an act of kindness should leave behind humiliation and rancour as that it should make the beneficiary grateful; we accept it as just as understandable that a declaration of love should produce indifference as that it should be reciprocated. There are countless similar cases.'[37]

At the risk of sounding flippant, then, one might say that the choice between hermeneutic and psychological understanding is between the indeterminate and the unverifiable. Simmel seems to have accepted this sceptical conclusion and, as Aron puts it: 'contents himself with a metaphysical consecration of, and literary comments on, the real difficulties, or only endows history with an expressive truth [*vérité d'expression*]'.[38]

Max Weber tried to bring psychological or motivational understanding, at least, within the pale of science. He took an eclectic view of the elaborate distinctions drawn by Dilthey, Rickert and Simmel. Although the concept of *Verstehen* is central to his sociology, he was concerned less with its philosophical rationale

---

[36] ibid., pp. 75f.   [37] ibid., p. 76.
[38] Aron, op. cit., p. 279.

than with its place in his own methodology. For Weber, the crucial fact was that 'the course of human action and human expressions of every sort are open to an interpretation in terms of meaning [*sinnvolle Deutung*] which in the case of other objects would have an analogy only on the level of metaphysics'.[39] He tends to treat this 'meaningful interpretation' (*sinnvolle Deutung*) or *Verstehen* as 'an unproblematic quantity',[40] neglecting in particular Rickert's crucial distinction between psychological and 'ideal' relations.[41]

As Aron rightly stresses: 'All Weber's efforts were directed to the following problem: under what conditions and within what limits can a judgement founded on understanding be said to be universally valid, that is, true?'[42] As a result, he was naturally drawn to the same problems which had preoccupied Karl Jaspers in his *Allgemeine Psychopathologie* of 1913,[43] the relation between the causal explanation of behaviour in terms of observable regularities and a 'genetic understanding' which empathetically perceives 'the meaning of psychic connections and the emergence of one psychic phenomenon from another', such as 'the anger of someone attacked, the jealousy of the man made cuckold, the acts and decisions that spring from motive'.[44]

Weber's distinction between 'direct' (*aktuelles*) and 'explanatory' (*erklärendes*) or *motivationsmässiges Verstehen* may well be borrowed from the one Jaspers drew between 'static understanding', meaning 'the presentation to oneself of psychic states, the objectifying to oneself of psychic qualities'[45] and 'genetic understanding'. But there is an important difference in the way in which they conceive the former process: Jaspers emphasises the phenomenological aspect, 'a feeling, an overtone, betokening the meaning, the sense of

[39] Weber, *GAW*, pp. 12–13n.

[40] von Schelting, op. cit., p. 323.

[41] Aron suggests an explanation of Weber's attitude: 'What is primary is the fact that there exist intelligible relations between historical events. Whether these relations are *philosophically* immanent in lived experience or transcend it, is unimportant. From a logical point of view, at any rate, it is as though these intelligible relationships were internal to reality itself. As a result understanding is, in Weber's eyes, simultaneously the understanding of meaning and of the psychic phenomenon,' Aron, op. cit., pp. 239f.

[42] ibid., p. 240.

[43] Karl Jaspers, *General Psychopathology* (English tr.) (Manchester University Press, 1962). See also E. Spranger, *Types of Men* (Halle, Niemayer, 3rd edn, 1928).

[44] Jaspers, op. cit., p. 27.

[45] ibid., p. 118.

the forms, their psyche',[46] while Weber treats 'direct understanding' as an unproblematic process, in which understanding the nature of a human expression (for instance of anger) or activity is essentially the same as grasping a logical or mathematical proposition.[47] It is this bland treatment of 'objective meanings' which has given rise to what may be called the 'phenomenological critique of Weber'. For the moment, however, I should like to concentrate on his discussion of motives and 'subjective meanings' and to show, with a few remarks about more recent approaches, that the analysis of motives can be treated as a separate issue which, despite the empirical difficulties which may exist, raises few conceptual problems.

I think it is fair to say that both what Weber calls *direct* understanding of the intended meaning of an action and what he calls *motivational* understanding operate at a level at which the 'objective meanings' of actions have already been taken for granted. Weber considers that it is the agent's subjective meaning which distinguishes action from mere behaviour,[48] but although this *may* coincide with the objective meaning of the action it is not clear that this need always be the case, even in relation to 'rational action',[49] at least if we take the 'objective meaning' to include some reference to the consequences of the action as they are known to an observer. In other words, though it may seem plausible to argue that we understand the action of someone inserting a bookmark by grasping his *intention*, this is to leave out a good deal of the story – in particular what it is that makes this action conceivable for the agent and recognisable by others.[50]

It should be noted that the analysis I am proposing rather goes against Weber's text. He rejects[51] the notion of an 'objectively correct' meaning as being relevant only to dogmatic disciplines such as jurisprudence, logic, ethics and aesthetics. Moreover, when he contrasts motivational or explanatory understanding with 'direct' understanding he assigns to the formeɪ type processes which I should

[46] loc. cit.

[47] M. Weber, *Economy and Society* (New York, Bedminster, 1968), p. 8.

[48] ibid., p. 4.

[49] In this case, Weber writes, the action acquires a 'meaningful structure' which we can understand. The example he gives is of a man chopping wood. If he is doing it for money or for his own requirements or for recreation, we understand it 'rationally'; if he is doing it to work off an emotional state, we understand it irrationally. He had earlier argued (*GAW*, p. 428) that interpretation in terms of instrumental rationality (*zweckrationale Deutung*) furnishes the most 'obvious' explanations.

[50] Weber, *GAW*, pp. 332ff.

[51] Weber, *Economy and Society*, p. 4.

be more inclined to see in terms of the latter.[52] I hope that this question will become clearer in the following pages. For the moment, at least, we are only concerned with the understanding of intentions and motives. This sort of understanding, Weber emphasises, does not conflict in any way with causal explanation; a *verstehende* interpretation is essentially a causal *hypothesis*. As such, its plausibility or *Evidenz* clearly does not make it 'the causally valid interpretation'.[53] He refers at this point to Simmel who noted, as we have seen, that two directly opposite emotional reactions to a 'stimulus' may be equally 'understandable'.

This view of *Verstehen* as an auxiliary process which serves only to generate hypotheses has been emphasised by Weber's positivist interpreters. Theodore Abel, for instance, understands *Verstehen* as the application of a 'behaviour maxim' derived from the observer's own experience which makes a 'relevant' connection between two or more observed phenomena. This helps in the 'preliminary explorations of a subject'; the application of the behaviour maxim is hypothetical. 'I cannot be certain that this is the *correct* or true explanation [of someone's conduct]. . . . I am certain only that my interpretation *could* be correct.'[54]

I shall discuss the problems of this view at a later stage. There is, however, another side to Weber's account of the relation of *Verstehen* to causal explanation which is less often mentioned by positivists; this is the claim that a causal explanation is deficient as a sociological explanation unless the process it purports to describe can be '*verstanden*':

> 'Our need for a causal explanation (*unser kausales Bedürfnis*) demands that where an "interpretation" (*Deutung*) is in principle possible, it be carried out; i.e. for the interpretation of human behaviour it is not sufficient for it to be related to a mere empirically observable law [*Regel des Geschehens*], however strict that law might be.'[55]

[52] '. . . we understand in terms of *motive* the meaning an actor attaches to the proposition twice two equals four, when he states it or writes it down, in that we understand what makes him do this at precisely this moment and in these circumstances. Understanding in this sense is attained if we know that he is engaged in balancing a ledger or in making a scientific demonstration, or is engaged in some other task of which this particular act would be an appropriate part. . . .' *Economy and Society*, p. 8.

[53] ibid., p. 9.

[54] T. Abel, 'The Operation Called *Verstehen*', *American Journal of Sociology*, Vol. 54 (1948).

[55] Weber, *GAW*, p. 69.

D

This requirement that human action should, wherever possible, be 'interpreted' rather than simply incorporated in a generalisation is one of the reasons for Weber's hostility to the idea of grounding sociology in some other science such as physiology or naturalistic psychology.[56] That a satisfactory sociological explanation must be understandable in this sense can be seen if we consider Alasdair MacIntyre's example of the proneness to suicide of people who live alone in bed-sitters:

> 'We still have to ask whether it is the pressure on the emotions of the isolation itself, or whether it is the insolubility of certain other problems in conditions of isolation which leads to suicide. Unless such questions about motives and reasons are answered, the causal generalisation "isolated living of a certain kind tends to lead to acts of suicide" is not so much an explanation in itself as an additional fact to be explained, even though it is a perfectly sound generalisation and even though to learn its truth might be to learn how the suicide rate could be increased or decreased in large cities by changing our housing policies.'[57]

None of this, of course, conflicts with the central positivist requirement, which is simply that *Verstehen* should not enter the criteria of validity of a causal generalisation; in the case above, it merely serves to introduce another set of causal questions. This is not to say, however, that if we take seriously the idea that the identification of a motivational connection is an essential part of causal explanation of human actions, the account of causality which derives ultimately from Hume may not turn out to be deficient.[58]

I shall not go into the relationship between Weber's account of motivation and discussions of the topic in modern analytic philosophy. Runciman has suggested that even if one takes the extreme view that motives are always logically and (therefore) never causally related to actions, 'The consequences for Weber's argument would be little more than verbal: what he calls (mistakenly, on this view) explanation in terms of motive should be called nothing more than the identification of the action (and its motive) which requires to be explained.'[59]

[56] Weber, *Economy and Society*, pp. 7f.

[57] A. MacIntyre, 'The Idea of a Social Science', *Proceedings of the Aristotelian Society* (supplementary volume, 1967), pp. 95–114.

[58] R. Harré and P. F. Secord, *The Explanation of Social Behaviour* (Oxford, Blackwell, 1972), is a very interesting attempt to break out of the apparently endless discussion of causes *v.* reasons, motives etc. and to work out a coherent methodology for explaining social behaviour.

[59] Runciman, op. cit., p. 27.

This may, in fact, be a more satisfactory way of describing the postulatory or ideal-typical accounts of motivation which Weber often gives. To describe these as motivational *hypotheses* is appropriate in some cases but not in all: the typology of action, in particular,[60] functions rather as a normative schema which is used to order the behavioural phenomena and which has a heuristic justification. Weber emphasises that action rarely conforms entirely to one of these 'pure types' of orientation:

> 'It would be very unusual to find concrete cases of action, especially of social action, which were orientated *only* in one or another of these ways. Furthermore, this classification of the modes of orientation of action is in no sense meant to exhaust the possibilities of the field, but only to formulate in conceptually clear form certain sociologically important types to which actual action is more or less closely approximated or in much the more common case, which constitute its elements. The usefulness of the classification for the purposes of this investigation can only be judged in terms of its results.'[61]

In other cases, of course, there is a more genuinely hypothetical element, as Runciman implies in his remarks on *Sinn-* and *Kausalad-äquanz*: ' "adequacy in terms of meaning" furnishes "explanatory understanding" where the complex of subjective meaning [*Sinnzusammenhang*] attributed to the agent is recognised by the

[60] 'Social action, like all action, may be orientated in four ways. It may be:
1. *instrumentally rational* [*zweckrational*] that is, determined by expectations as to the behaviour of objects in the environment and of other human beings; these expectations are used as "conditions" or "means" for the attainment of the actor's own rationally pursued and calculated ends;
2. *value-rational* [*wertrational*] that is, determined by a conscious belief in the value for its own sake of some ethical, aesthetic, religious or other form of behaviour, independently of its prospects of success;
3. *affectual* (especially emotional), that is, determined by the actor's specific affects and feeling states;
4. *traditional*, that is, determined by ingrained habituation.'
(*Economy and Society*, pp. 24f.)
[61] *Economy and Society*, p. 26. Cf. *GAW*, p. 131 (reprinted in A. Giddens (ed.), *Positivism and Sociology* (London, Heinemann, 1974), p. 26). 'Such schemes of interpretation [i.e. the interpretation of human actions in terms of purposes, motives, means etc.] . . . are not merely, as has been said, "hypotheses" analogous to scientific hypothetical "laws". They can function as hypotheses in a heuristic sense for the interpretation of concrete events. But, contrary to scientific hypotheses, the statement that they do not in any concrete case contain a valid interpretation, does not impugn their interpretative value. . . .'

observer, who can therefore deduce from it the consequences which
will follow *if* the agent acts consistently in terms of it'.[62]

Although it may be 'in part, at least, a verbal issue at what point
the identification of an action slides over into its explanation',[63] it
is clear that the latter presupposes the former, and it is the understanding of meaning to which we must now turn. These questions
arise at two ostensibly different levels in Weber's methodology:
firstly, the identification of actions by direct understanding (which,
in Weber's eyes, is still understanding of *subjective meaning*); and
secondly, the high-level understanding of complex intellectual
structures (*Geistesgebilde*). These two processes can, I think, be
shown to be related aspects of a single operation—the construction
of theoretical concepts by abstraction from a range of data.

I have already discussed Weber's concept of *aktuelles Verstehen*
and the way he treats this activity as something essentially
unproblematic. More recent research, especially in anthropology,
has made social scientists much more aware of the difficulties
involved in accurately describing the actions of people in 'alien
cultures'.[64] But Weber's commentators, notably von Schelting and
Parsons, have emphasised that Weber's substantive works also
make use of a kind of understanding which is never more than hinted
at in his methodological writings.[65] Besides the 'causal' understanding of motives there is what von Schelting calls, rather
alarmingly, the acausal-ideal understanding of concrete meaning
structures' (*konkrete Sinngebilde*). The best example of this is
Weber's concept of the 'spirit of capitalism', a complex whole which
gives meaning to the various beliefs and actions of which it is made
up.

Although Weber's *Protestant Ethic*[66] aimed ultimately to provide
a causal explanation of the rise of capitalism (or at the very least a
complementary causal explanation to that provided by historical
materialism), von Schelting shows that in order to give more than a
purely extrinsic account of the correlations between 'capitalist'
economic innovation and certain forms of Protestantism, Weber

[62] Runciman, op. cit., p. 44.

[63] ibid., p. 42; cf. Aron, op. cit., pp. 252f.

[64] See, especially P. Winch, *The Idea of a Social Science* (London, Routledge,
1958), also the exchange in the *Archives Européenes de Sociologie* (1967) between
Steven Lukes, Martin Hollis and John Torrance.

[65] Von Schelting, op. cit., p. 327n.

[66] M. Weber, *The Protestant Ethic and the Spirit of Capitalism*, tr. T. Parsons
(London, Allen & Unwin, 1971).

had to go beyond the limits of what he called 'motivational' and Jaspers called 'genetic' understanding. Simplifying considerably: motivational understanding would have been sufficient to grasp the connection between the Protestant ethic and the spirit of capitalism only if the former had contained explicit economic prescriptions of the appropriate type, if the message of the Protestant divines had been an unambiguous *enrichissez-vous*. In fact, of course, the opposite was the case; as Weber emphasised in the introduction to his monograph: 'If any inner relationship between certain expressions of the old Protestant spirit and modern capitalistic culture is to be found, we must attempt to find it in its purely religious characteristics.'[67]

The meaning-relations which make up the complex whole of the 'Protestant ethic' are not only logical relations of implication. Often, indeed, they seem at first sight paradoxical. The Calvinist doctrine of predestination, for example, considered on its own, would seem to indicate fatalism rather than devotion to controlled economic activity. The conceptual link with the latter can only be established by considering the larger 'context of meaning' which would include, in this case, the Calvinist concept of God.[68]

The relation of this sort of understanding or interpretation to causal explanation is by no means as clear as in the case of *Motivationsverstehen*. As Aron put it:

> 'once one has completed the interpretation of a whole way of life in terms of a religious or ethical system, there is no longer any question of subsequent causal verification (since it is quite a different question to know how effective was Protestantism in furthering the rise of capitalism). The requirement of causality means only that the interpretation must rethink men as they were, as they really lived—an obvious requirement internal to any understanding and different from the *a posteriori* causality which is external to understanding and which is established by means of hypotheses and probabilistic reasoning.'[69]

Of course the positivist concept of cause which Aron invokes is not the only possible one. If, like Harré and Secord, we understand causal explanation to involve the identification of *causal mechanisms* it seems not unlikely that these should include such things as 'the meanings [people] assign to items in their human environment' and

[67] ibid., p. 45.
[68] Von Schelting, op. cit., p. 393. Cf. M. Weber, *Religionssoziologie* (*RS*) (Tübingen, Mohr, 1928), Vol. I, pp. 111f.
[69] Aron, op. cit., p. 265.

'the rules and conventions they follow in monitoring their social behaviour' etc.[70] But Aron's point can be made in another way if we consider the distinction between the 'subjective' and the 'objective' meaning of actions. Social science cannot do without general concepts which are not reducible in any simple way to the conceptions and interpretations of individual agents. It is true that Weber sometimes attempts to confine his definitions to the subjective interpretations of individuals,[71] but he also favours definitions in terms of objective probabilities which clearly are not part of the subjective *sens vécu* of the agents.[72] Protestantism, in Weber's sense,

> 'transcends individual consciousness; it was never lived in this way by any individual; it appears as the formalisation and elucidation of the more or less obscure or implicit thought of historical agents[73] . . . if then the meaning which corresponds to the internal logic of conduct is already objective and not subjective, then Weber, without intending to, has created a science of objective meanings. In fact the "lived meaning" to which sociology refers cannot be purely individual. The spirit of a religion or of a legal system is a part of historical reality, without being assimilable to the experiences of individual consciousness.'[74]

The conceptual structures, such as the 'spirit' of an economic system or of a legal code, cheerfully postulated by thinkers of Weber's generation (and respectfully treated by Aron) have been largely abandoned (despite a partial rehabilitation here and there in terms of modern 'structuralism'). However, the same problem of the

[70] Harré and Secord, op. cit., p. 174.

[71] 'When we ask what corresponds to the idea of the "State" in empirical reality, we find an infinity of diffuse and discrete human actions and passions . . . all held together by an idea—the belief in norms and relations of authority of men over men which are or ought to be binding.' (*GAW*, p. 200; E. Shils and H. A. Finch, *The Philosophy of the Social Sciences* (Glencoe, Free Press, 1949), p. 99. Quoted by Runciman, op. cit., p. 29n.)

[72] Aron, op. cit., pp. 243f. See, for example, the definition of 'social relationship' in *Economy and Society*: 'The social relationship . . . consists entirely and exclusively in the existence of a probability that there will be a meaningful course of social action. . . .' (*Economy and Society*, pp. 26f.)

[73] Cf. Weber's remark on Hindu religion: 'For the practical effect in which we are interested it is of no importance that the individual pious Hindu did not always have before his eyes, as a total system, the pathetic presuppositions of the Karma doctrine which transformed the world into a strictly rational and ethically determined cosmos. He remained confined to the cage which only made sense through this ideal system [*Zusammenhang*], and the consequences weighed down upon his action.' (*RS*, Vol. II, pp. 120ff.—quoted by von Schelting, op. cit., p. 386.)

[74] Aron, op. cit., p. 307.

understanding of meaning (*Sinnverstehen*) arises in the initial conceptualisation of social phenomena. Weber oversimplified this problem of 'direct understanding'; the phenomenological critique, as we shall see, reconstructs these 'objective meanings' in terms of a multiplicity of subjective interpretations.

5

Verstehen and Dialectic

So far as there exists a coherent *'verstehende'* or *'geisteswissenschaft-liche'* tradition around the works of Dilthey, Rickert, Simmel and to some extent Weber, it has been, as one might expect, uncongenial to most Marxist thinkers. They tend to object to: (*a*) its contemplative character, which it shares with historicism in general; and (*b*) its idealism, the tendency to collapse history into the history of thought (*Geistesgeschichte*).

It is worth noting that the first charge can be pressed even on strictly Hegelian principles. Hans-Georg Gadamer[1] has argued, with reference to Hegel's discussion of the 'religion of art' in the *Phenomenology of Mind*, that hermeneutic reconstruction of the historical context of cultural products is an 'external activity' (*äusserliches Tun*) which aims to represent objects as they are 'in themselves' (*an sich*); the *subject* of knowledge is not changed in the process. For Hegel, writes Gadamer, hermeneutic problems are only resolved at a higher level, the level of philosophy or the mind's historical understanding of itself. 'This is the extreme opposite of the self-forgetfulness of the historical consciousness. The historical attitude of representation is replaced by a thinking attitude to the past . . . not the restitution of what is past, but a thinking mediation with present life.'[2]

The second objection, to what I have loosely called the 'idealism' of the *Geisteswissenschaft* tradition, is more obvious. Hans Georg Gadamer, himself no Marxist, writes that the aim of his investigation of the philosophy of history of Droysen and Dilthey was:

[1] H.-G. Gadamer, *Wahrheit und Methode* (Tübingen, Mohr, 2nd edn, 1965).
[2] ibid., p. 101.

'to show that despite all the Historical School's opposition to Hegel's spiritualism their hermeneutic approach led them to read history like a book, i.e. as something which was meaningful down to the last letter. For all his protests against a philosophy of history in which the necessity of the concept makes up the essence of everything that happens, Dilthey's historical hermeneutic did not avoid making history culminate in the history of the mind [*Geistesgeschichte*].'[3]

The *Geisteswissenschaft* tradition which popularised the concept of *Verstehen* was undoubtedly close to philosophical idealism in many ways, (although one can also find, especially in Dilthey and Simmel, a strong emphasis on material reality, albeit expressed in a rather incoherent *Lebensphilosophie*). As we have seen, both Droysen and Dilthey explicitly opposed both positivism and and materialism, though one should not forget that what was understood by the latter was not often anything that Marx would have recognised.[4] The main burden of the Marxist charge—that the *Geisteswissenschaft* tradition neglected the importance of 'real factors' in social life and tended to search for 'deeper' interpretations of phenomena which were better suited to a causal explanation—is easily sustained, but such arguments are not peculiar to Marxism. Some recent critiques of a *verstehende* approach, whether directed mainly against Weber or against 'phenomenological sociology', have tended to presuppose a coherent Marxist theory of knowledge which (despite the interesting results of the curious marriage of Marxism and traditional French *épistémologie*) cannot yet be said to exist.[5] It is not clear, however, that a moderate *verstehende* position such as Max Weber's need directly conflict with the requirements of Marxist theory.

One of the most serious attempts to mediate between the two traditions is that of the Austrian Marxist, Max Adler (1873–1937). Adler was concerned to provide Marxism with a solid epistemological foundation which he conceived in Kantian terms. A late work, *The*

[3] ibid., p. xxi.

[4] Cf. Giddens's comment that 'Weber's views upon the validity and usefulness of Marx's original work . . . have to be partially disentangled from his assessment of "vulgar" Marxism.' A. Giddens, *Capitalism and Modern Social Theory* (Cambridge University Press, 1971), p. 193.

[5] See, for example, B. Hindess, *The Use of Official Statistics in Sociology* (London, Macmillan, 1973). For an earlier Marxist and logical positivist attack on *verstehende* sociology, see O. Neurath, *Empiricism and Sociology*, pp. 353–8.

Riddle of Society,[6] incorporates important elements of the theory of
Verstehen into its 'epistemological groundwork of social science'.

In the introduction, entitled 'Why Sociology Must Begin with
Epistemology', Adler insisted that society has a reality of its own, and
must not be treated naturalistically. 'The social' is not, however, a
category of 'naïve consciousness': 'What appears to be immediately
given is only a multiplicity of men acting in different ways with and
against one another, whom we all conceive, by analogy with our-
selves, as individuals.'[7] There is also, however, a 'social *a priori*'
which can be identified by critical reflection and which makes
possible not just our knowledge of social life, but social life itself.

According to Adler, much of the discussion of problems of
Verstehen in previous decades had been really a halting and confused
approach towards the 'transcendental-social' position which he had
been advocating 'since 1904'.[8] There are, he claimed, two theories of
Verstehen. The first is a matter of hermeneutics, of philological and
psychological interpretation; when Sombart claimed (at the Sixth
Conference of German Sociologists in 1928[9]) that the theory of
understanding was already completely worked out by the end of the
nineteenth century he must have had in mind this sort of understanding. But there is also an epistemological theory of understanding[10] in
which it functions as a transcendental concept underlying all our
social experience.

This second concept of understanding has not, Adler says, been
fully worked out. Most previous discussions of the question, such as
Weber's, concentrate on methodological and psychological observa-
tions on the character and the limits of understanding, or hermeneutic questions about the validity of interpretations, or finally
logical discussions of the relationship between understanding and
explanation. These questions are, of course, all relevant to the
'problem of understanding', but only secondarily, since 'they all
presuppose the concept and thereby the fact of understanding, i.e.
the fact of a characteristic operation of consciousness . . .'.[11]

[6] Max Adler, *Das Rätsel der Gesellschaft: Zur erkenntniskritischen Grundlegung der Sozialwissenschaft* (Vienna, Saturn-Verlag, 1936).
[7] ibid., p. 28.
[8] ibid., p. 203; 1904 is the date of Adler's first major work, *Kausalität und Teleologie im Streite um die Wissenschaft*.
[9] *Verhandlungen des 6 deutschen Soziologentages*.
[10] Adler, *Das Rätsel der Gesellschaft*, pp. 141, 147.
[11] ibid., p. 142.

This operation of understanding seems unproblematic only from an uncritical perspective, for its essence involves a 'curious departure by the ego from and beyond itself which amounts to a union with other egos or with unknown mental contents'.[12] This process involves the grasp of a *meaning* and is essentially social in character (and not, as it is often portrayed, a private, individual matter). Understanding is not 'irrational', nor is it as radically different from causal explanation as is often believed:

'It is misleading when some writers such as Jaspers and Sombart present these two concepts as mutually exclusive. Explanation means the reduction of an event to its causes. But understanding is then only a particular sort of causal explanation; Max Weber was therefore quite right to say that understanding and causal explanation are ultimately connected and that in the cultural sphere [*im geistigen Gebiete*] we "explain through understanding". What is important is that each constitutes a different method of explanation, the choice between which does not however depend on the whim of the investigator but on the fact that there are different types of causality, natural, organic and psychic. . . . Understanding will reveal itself as the specific causal explanation for those forms of being in which the individual [*das Einzelne*] is only possible in virtue of a totality to which it belongs as a member, i.e. for organic and social being.'[13]

For Adler, then, this epistemological concept of understanding leads to the more general concept of 'social being', which he seems to equate with the individual's awareness of his social nature. 'The individual consciousness is *a priori* socialised.'[14]

This position may be compared with that expressed in Simmel's essay 'How is Society Possible?'[15] Simmel's answer to the question is, briefly, that the process Kant described whereby the human intellect shapes and orders sense-perceptions into a coherent picture of 'nature' can function as a model for the way in which a society is made up of individuals.

'However, there is a decisive difference between the unity of society and the unity of nature. It is this: In the Kantian view (which we follow here) the unity of nature emerges in the observing subject exclusively; it is produced exclusively by him in the sense materials, and on the basis of

12 loc. cit.
13 ibid., p. 148.
14 ibid., p. 178.
15 Georg Simmel: *Essays on Sociology, Philosophy and Aesthetics*, edited by Kurt Wolff (New York, Harper & Row, 1965).

sense materials, which are in themselves heterogeneous. By contrast, the unity of society needs no observer. It is directly realised by its own elements because these elements are themselves conscious and synthesising units . . . the consciousness of constituting with the others a unity is actually all there is to this unity.'[16]

Though this formulation seems strikingly close to Adler's views, he in fact takes a critical view of it. He praises Simmel for asking the right question, namely 'what are the *a priori* preconditions for the fact that ". . . particular, concrete processes in the *individual* consciousness are actually processes of *sociation*? Which elements in them account for the fact that (to put it abstractly) their achievement is the production of a societal unit out of individuals?" '[17] But he considers that Simmel's attempt to answer the question does no more than reveal the '*psychological* preconditions of social interaction'.[18]

Only in Simmel's later article on the nature of historical understanding, which has already been discussed, does Adler consider that he has achieved a correct account of the problem. The first and most basic sort of understanding which Simmel identifies there is the recognition of 'other minds'. It is not, he argues, a matter of knowing that one has a mind oneself and imputing one to other suitable bodies; rather, the 'You', or 'the Other understood directly as endowed with a mind'[19] is a fundamental datum, 'a basic phenomenon of the human spirit'. Adler cites with approval the following passage: 'The "You" and understanding are the same, expressed in the one case as a substance and in the other as a function . . . it is the transcendental basis for the fact that man is a *zoon politikon*.'[20]

I have tried to concentrate on the concept of *Verstehen* as a *method*, rather than discuss in detail these general epistemological and ontological questions. Yet something should be said about these ideas, which have come up explicitly or implicitly throughout the present investigation.[21] Much philosophical effort has been expounded on the 'problem of other minds', but many people at least would now agree that the 'person' is a primary concept out of which

[16] ibid., p. 338.   [17] Adler, op. cit., p. 205.
[18] loc. cit.

[19] G. Simmel, '*Vom Wesen des historischen Verstehens*', *Brücke und Tür* (Stuttgart, Koehler, 1957), p. 67.

[20] ibid. p. 68, quoted by Adler, op. cit., p. 207.

[21] Cf. Droysen's concept of understanding as a 'basic element of human existence' (p. 22 above) and phenomenological analyses by Scheler, Heidegger and Sartre.

'mind' and 'body' are later abstracted analytically, and secondly that to have the concept 'person' involves being able to recognise oneself as one person among others.[22] To this extent, at least, recent thought tends to support Simmel and Adler. But they were also arguing something much more radical, namely that one can identify the transcendental conditions necessary for the existence of human societies, and in Adler's case, that one must have an ontological concept of a 'social being' which is radically different from 'natural being' (i.e. the world of natural objects).

It is difficult to know how to understand such a claim. One should recognise that most systems of social thought are grounded in some sort of implicit 'ontology of the social'; to compare, say, Durkheim's fundamental assumptions about society with Weber's would be enough to bring this out. One should therefore give credit to thinkers who try to make their presuppositions explicit, but a full-scale philosophical justification of such presuppositions would be a Herculean task which Adler and Simmel cannot be said to have achieved. Very briefly, I would suggest that while Adler's stress on what Durkheim called the '*sui generis* reality of society' is legitimate, the notion of a transcendental theory of the social is highly questionable; as Adler presents it, this adds an unnecessarily speculative flavour to his account. The questions which his 'epistemological' or 'transcendental' concept of understanding is designed to tackle do not in fact demand such an answer; while they are not psychological questions, they can properly be treated as hermeneutic ones. In other words, the question why social life and the behaviour of other people is in some sense intelligible to us need not be discussed in terms of an *a priori* 'social' form of apperception; it is enough to say that we live in the same world as our fellow men and have a certain amount in common with them. Adler comes close to recognising this when he writes that the social is a 'form of consciousness' which is also a 'form of *being*' (*Seinsform*) and that 'the *individual* consciousness is *a priori* socialised'.[23]

Adler emphasises that the means by which mutual understanding is attained (e.g. language) are social in character and so 'from an epistemological point of view ... the limits of understanding coincide with the limits of social experience'.[24] One should not, therefore, he implies, think of our understanding as limited by some 'unfathomable

[22] See, in particular, P. F. Strawson, *Individuals* (London, Methuen, 1959).
[23] Adler, op. cit., p. 178.
[24] ibid., p. 153.

remnant of the ego'[25] but attend rather to the practical limits of understanding revealed by, for instance, Marxism and psychoanalysis. 'Marxism . . . has shown how far scientific knowledge and the understanding of men and works which it provides (*vermittelt*) depends, unbeknown to the researcher, on his class position. . . .'[26] Similarly, he argues, psychoanalysis has shown the impossibility of complete understanding between man and wife: neither can experience directly what it is to belong to the opposite sex.[27]

This view of Marxism is not as limited as it might appear; much of Jürgen Habermas's recent work has discussed psychoanalysis and '*Ideologiekritik*' (the criticism of ideology in Marxist terms) as twin approaches to the study and interpretation of 'systematically distorted communication'. I shall discuss Habermas in detail in a later chapter, but it may be helpful to say something at this point about the 'Frankfurt school' of 'critical theory', of which Habermas is a second-generation representative. This theoretical movement grew up in the 1920s and 30s around the Frankfurt *Institut für Sozialforschung* (Institute of Social Research).[28] Its central figures were Max Horkheimer, who directed it from 1930 until 1958, Theodor Adorno, co-author with Horkheimer of the *Dialectic of Enlightenment*, the economist Friedrich Pollock, the sociologist of literature and culture Leo Lowenthal and, perhaps best known, Herbert Marcuse. The institute emigrated to the USA after Hitler's rise to power and returned in 1950 (though without Lowenthal and Marcuse). Its theoretical position, despite individual differences of emphasis, is best described as a highly sophisticated neo-Marxism with strong Kantian and Hegelian elements—in other words, a Marxism which saw the German idealist tradition as still crucially important.

Both Horkheimer and Marcuse seem to have been influenced by the '*Geisteswissenschaft*' tradition, especially Dilthey. Horkheimer wrote a wide-ranging and broadly sympathetic article on 'The Relation between Psychology and Sociology in the Work of Wilhelm Dilthey',[29] although he suggested that Dilthey had not fully realised how limited a contribution psychological understanding could make to the writing of history. Even Dilthey's *Lebensphilosophie* was less

[25] ibid., p. 151.   [26] ibid., p. 149.
[27] ibid., p. 150.
[28] For the history of the institute, and a sensitive discussion of its work, see Martin Jay, *The Dialectical Imagination* (London, Heinemann, 1973).
[29] *Studies in Philosophy and Social Science*, Vol. VIII, No. 3 (1939).

offensive to Horkheimer than to most other Marxist writers.[30] Marcuse's debt to Dilthey can be seen in an article on 'The Problem of Historical Reality'[31] and in his *Habilitationsschrift, Hegel's Ontology and the Foundation of a Theory of Historicity.*[32]

Jürgen Habermas returned to the same themes in his reflections on positivism in the social sciences. As he put it at the beginning of *Zur Logik der Sozialwissenschaften*:[33] 'There would be no reason to disturb the concealed complex of scientific dualism [*Wissenschafts-dualismus*], if it did not repeatedly lead in one sphere to symptoms which require an analytic solution: the sphere of the social sciences is marked by the collision and interpenetration of heterogeneous approaches and aims.'[34] Habermas's own attempt to do justice to the claims of both '*Verstehen*' and '*Erklären*' will be discussed later.

Before going on to discuss other Marxist writers, it may be helpful to attempt some theoretical distinctions. It is extremely difficult to determine whether and to what extent a writer uses a *verstehende* approach. One can perhaps distinguish three elements of such an approach, though often they will go together and reinforce one another.

1. A general hostility to positivism, stressing the distinctiveness of the human sciences or, more generally, of 'the social'. There will tend to be associated with this a particular epistemological and methodo- logical position on the way in which one can obtain access to data in this realm, e.g. by empathy, re-experiencing (*Nacherleben*) or imaginative reconstruction.
2. A stress on the usefulness of teleological explanations of human behaviour, as opposed to explanations cast purely in terms of efficient causes. This can be expressed in terms of the Marxist notion of 'praxis' and, in Sartre's terminology, 'project'.[35]

[30] Cf. Jay, op. cit., p. 49. On *Lebensphilosophie*, see Ch. 3, n. 6 above.

[31] '*Das Problem der geschichtlichen Realität*', *Die Gesellschaft*, Vol. VIII, No. 4 (1931); cited by Jay, op. cit., p. 73.

[32] *Hegels Ontologie und die Grundlegung einer Theorie der Geschichtlichkeit* (Frankfurt, Klostermann, 1968), first pub. 1932.

[33] Jürgen Habermas, *Zur Logik der Sozialwissenschaften* (Frankfurt, Suhrkamp 2nd edn, 1971).

[34] ibid., p. 72.

[35] J.-P. Sartre, *Critique de la raison dialectique* (précédé de *Question de méthode*) (Paris, Gallimard, 1960), passim. The prefatory essay is available in English under the title *The Problem of Method* (London, Methuen, 1963) to which I refer here ('tr').

3. The concept of 'form' or 'structure'. This element is perhaps rather less central, though it is emphasised by L. Goldmann, who derived it from Lukács and, he claims, from Hegel and Marx as well. Lukács and Goldmann are best known for their analyses of literature, though both of them also wrote extensively on more general theoretical questions. Goldmann, in particular, saw no essential difference between applying Marxist method to literature and using it to investigate other areas of life.

Max Adler, as we have seen, concentrated on the first aspect, the distinction between 'natural' and 'social' being. This seems at first sight to conflict with Marx's position, though the conflict is probably more apparent than real. Marx's ideal of 'one science', embracing both natural science and the 'science of man' did not mean the subordination of the latter to the former. There *are* positivistic elements in Marx's thought[36] and his 'system' was of course often interpreted by later Marxists in an excessively deterministic and mechanistic way. But Marx also placed great emphasis on man's creative interaction with nature[37] and on human activity or praxis.

It is this second theme which Sartre emphasises most, though he also argues the distinctiveness of the cultural from the natural world. 'What we call freedom is the irreducibility of the cultural to the natural order.'[38] His concept of the 'project' is a reformulation of the notion of 'praxis':

'We affirm the specificity of the human act, which cuts across the social *milieu* while still holding on to its determinations and which transforms the world on the basis of given conditions. For us man is characterised above all by his going beyond a situation, and by what he succeeds in making of what he has been made—even if he never recognises himself in his objectification. . . . The most rudimentary behaviour must be determined both in relation to the real and present factors which condition it and in relation to a certain object, still to come, which it is trying to bring into being. This is what we call the *project*.'[39]

[36] This question is interestingly discussed by Jürgen Habermas in his *Knowledge and Human Interests* (London, Heinemann, 1971); and by Albrecht Wellmer in his *Critical Theory of Society* (New York, Herder & Herder, 1971), especially Ch. 2.
[37] See Alfred Schmidt, *The Concept of Nature in Marx* (London, New Left Books, 1971).
[38] Sartre, op. cit., tr., p. 152.
[39] ibid., tr., p. 91.

Sartre refers explicitly to the traditional concept of *Verstehen*:

'Man is, for himself and for others, a signifying being, since one can never understand the slightest of his gestures without going beyond the pure present and explaining it by the future. . . .
    To grasp the meaning of any human conduct, it is necessary to have at our disposal what German psychiatrists and historians have called "comprehension". But what is involved here is neither a particular talent nor a special faculty of intuition; this knowing is simply the dialectical movement which explains the act by its terminal signification in terms of its starting conditions. It is essentially progressive.'[40]

What Sartre seems to be thinking of here is an account of human action in teleological terms.[41] He goes on:

'If my companion suddenly starts toward the window, I understand his gesture in terms of the material situation in which we both are. It is, for example, because the room is too warm. He is going "to let in some air". This action is not inscribed in the temperature; it is not "set in motion" by the warmth or by a "stimulus" provoking chain reactions. There is present here a synthetic conduct which, by unifying itself, unifies before my eyes the practical field in which we both are. . . .'[42]

'. . . The movement of comprehension is simultaneously progressive (toward the objective result) and regressive (I go back toward the original condition.'[43]

Sartre has already argued[44] that

'the qualities of external determination and those of that synthetic, progressive unity which is human praxis are found inseparably connected in Marxist thought. . . .
    'If one wants to grant Marxist thought its full complexity, one would have to say that man in a period of exploitation is *at once both* the product of his own product and a historical agent who can under no circumstances be taken as a product.'[45]

This attitude, he suggests, may be 'the most profound theoretical contribution of Marxism'.[46]

---

[40] ibid., tr., p. 152.
[41] On teleological explanations of behaviour, see in particular Charles Taylor, *The Explanation of Behaviour* (London, Routledge, 1964), and G. H. von Wright, *Explanation and Understanding* (London, Routledge, 1971).
[42] Sartre, op. cit., tr., p. 153.
[43] ibid., tr., p. 154.   [44] ibid., tr., p. 87n.
[45] ibid., tr., p. 87.   [46] loc. cit.

E

Much of the *Critique de la raison dialectique* is concerned with how far the projects of social groups and in particular the working class can be 'understood' in this way. More generally, the whole work has the programmatic air of complementing both Marxism ('*l'indé-passable philosophie de notre temps*')[47] *and* positivist sociology with a 'structural anthropology' conceived in *verstehende* terms.

The lacuna which Sartre finds in Marxism is not easy to specify, especially in view of his remarks quoted above. Often he speaks elliptically of its neglect of the 'human dimension'[48] or just of 'man'.[49] What he means can, however, be seen in his criticisms of Marxist historiography and literary criticism. To cite one of the best-known passages:

> 'Valéry is a *petit bourgeois* intellectual, no doubt about it. But not every *petit bourgeois* intellectual is Valéry. The heuristic inadequacy of con-temporary Marxism is contained in these two sentences. Marxism lacks any hierarchy of mediations which would permit it to grasp the process which produces the person and his product inside a class and within a given society at a given historical moment. Characterising Valéry as a *petit bourgeois* and his work as idealist, the Marxist will find in both alike only what he has put there. . . . Marxism situates but no longer discovers anything.'[50]

In general, then, Marxism 'totalises' prematurely, whether in 'situating' Valéry or Flaubert or in equating the intentions of historical agents with the objective consequences of their actions. 'The original thought of Marx, as we find it in the *18th Brumaire*, attempts a difficult synthesis of intention and result; the contemporary use of that thought is superficial and dishonest.'[51] I cannot attempt here to give the *Critique* the detailed discussion it would require. In general, it seems that while much of what Sartre says about the inadequacy of contemporary Marxism is justified, these objections do not necessarily apply to a substantial body of Marxist thought which he tends to neglect. As Lucien Goldmann has written:

> 'If it is true that Marxism became for a certain time, in a very large number of works which invoked it, a mechanistic positivism, idealist or eclectic, the dialectical positions which Sartre defends, based on the concepts of *project*, or *primacy of the future*, of the *identity of subject and*

[47] ibid., p. 9; tr., p. xxxiv.   [48] ibid., tr., p. 181.
[49] ibid., tr., p. 179.   [50] ibid., pp. 44f.; tr., pp. 56f.
[51] ibid., p. 38; tr., p. 45.

object . . . existed already implicitly or explicitly in the work of Marx himself and in a whole sector of post-Marxian Marxist thought, especially from the time of Lukács's work of 1921.'[52]

Nor, as Goldmann complains, is it clear how Sartre's 'structural anthropology', which he never discusses except in very general terms,[53] would miraculously remove the inadequacies of positivist sociology,[54] by incorporating it as an 'auxiliary discipline'. Goldmann makes the extremely important point that:

'The fundamental methodological problem of any human science— above all if one places oneself in a structuralist and historical perspective —lies in the division [*découpage*] of the object of study and, in this particular case, in the delineation of meaningful structures.

'Once this division has been made and accepted, the results of the research will be practically predictable. . . .'

Sartre's position is close to what sociologists, following Parsons, have come to call the 'action frame of reference'. As we saw in discussing Max Weber, two fundamental problems remain in this context:

1. the identification of the 'subjective' meanings of action for the agent (the problem of psychological understanding);
2. the identification of the 'objective meaning' of those actions, and the way in which these meanings come to be laid down and understood in a human community (the problem of the 'hermeneutic' understanding of meaning). It is these 'objective meanings' which tend to be forced into an *a priori* normative schema, which may be flexible, as in Weber's typology of action, or more rigid, as in Parsons's 'pattern-variable dilemmas'.

Sartre's critique of positivist social science is hinted at, in his critical remarks about Kardiner, rather than argued in detail. Lukács, in his essay on 'Reification',[55] and Goldmann in *The Human Sciences and Philosophy*,[56] provide a rather more detailed analysis. Lukács

[52] Lucien Goldmann, *Marxisme et sciences humaines* (Paris, Gallimard, 1970), p. 246.
[53] See, e.g. Sartre, op. cit., pp. 104–8.
[54] Goldmann, op. cit., pp. 250f.
[55] 'Reification and the Consciousness of the Proletariat' in G. Lukács, *History and Class Consciousness* (London, Merlin Press, 1971).
[56] Lucien Goldmann, *The Human Sciences and Philosophy* (London, Cape, 1969).

argues that in a society where the commodity form is dominant and the division of labour most advanced:

'The specialisation of skills leads to the destruction of every image of the whole . . . the more intricate a modern science becomes and the better it understands itself methodologically, the more resolutely it will turn its back on the ontological problems of its own sphere of influence and eliminate them from the realm where it has achieved some insight. The more highly developed it becomes and the more scientific, the more it will become a formally closed system of partial laws. It will then find that the world lying beyond its confines, and in particular the material base which it is our task to understand, *its own concrete underlying reality lies*, methodologically and in principle, *beyond its grasp*.

Marx acutely summed up this situation with reference to economics when he declared that "use-value as such lies outside the sphere of investigation of political economy".'[57]

Human relations, Lukács argues, are assimilated to natural laws:

'All human relations (viewed as the objects of social activity) assume increasingly the objective form of the abstract elements of the conceptual systems of natural science and of the abstract substrata of the laws of nature. And also, the subject of this "action" likewise assumes increasingly the attitude of the pure observer of these—artificially abstract—processes, the attitude of the experimenter.'[58]

Goldmann's theoretical position is largely derived from that of Lukács, whose *History and Class Consciousness* he called 'a true encyclopedia of the human sciences'.[59] Goldmann writes:

'On the one hand, the historical and human sciences[60] are not, like the physico-chemical sciences, the study of a collection of facts *external* to men or of a world *upon which* their action bears. On the contrary, they are the study of *this action itself*, of its structure, of the aspirations which enliven it and the changes that it undergoes. On the other hand, since consciousness is only one *real*, but *partial* aspect of human activity, historical study does not have the right to limit itself to conscious phenomena; it must connect the conscious intentions of the actors of history to the objective meaning of their behaviour and actions.'[61]

[57] Lukács, op. cit., pp. 103f.
[58] ibid., p. 131.
[59] Goldmann, *The Human Sciences and Philosophy*, p. 44.
[60] Goldmann has already argued (ibid., p. 23) that 'Every social fact is a historical fact and vice versa. . . . Sociology cannot be concrete unless it is historical, just as history, if it wishes to go beyond the mere recording of facts, must necessarily become explicative, that is to say, more or less sociological.'
[61] ibid., p. 35.

It follows, he goes on, that 'When it is a question of studying human life, the process of *scientific knowing, since it is itself a human historical and social fact*, implies *the partial identity of the subject and object of* knowledge.'[62] Goldmann later, as we shall see, expresses that distinction between 'explanation' and 'understanding' in structural terms. Both, he argues, are implied by a Marxist analysis, and Marxism is a 'genetic structuralism':

'From an historical point of view, genetic structuralism appeared, it seems to me, for the first time as a fundamental philosophical idea with Hegel and Marx, although neither explicitly used this term. Nevertheless Hegelian and Marxist thought constitute, for the first time in the history of philosophy, rigorously monistic, structuralist and genetic positions. ... *Capital* might appear a static analysis in so far as it aims to illuminate the internal functioning of a capitalist society consisting only of employees and bosses . . . [But] . . . *Capital* is not a work of political economy, but, as even its title implies, a critique of political economy. It aims to show that economic phenomena as such are limited historical realities which appeared at a certain moment of development and which are destined to disappear in the course of future changes, phenomena characterised in the first place by the appearance within social life in general of an autonomous sector which acts more and more intensively and effectively on the others while being less and less influenced by them. In this sense and as long as this sector exists, economic facts have a relatively autonomous character and even an *explanatory* value for the study of phenomena which occur in other areas of social life; but it is precisely in this perspective that the genesis of economic life could not itself be economic in character. Marx is therefore entirely consistent when he shows that the capitalist system in which the economy functions as a relatively autonomous reality could only have been created by violence and can only be transcended by non-economic processes. . . .'[63]

Goldmann's characteristic interpretation of Marxism is never, to my mind, fully worked out. What he means by a 'genetic structuralism which is both interpretative [*compréhensif*] and explanatory'[64] is made somewhat clearer when he refers to Freud:

'Freud's central idea was precisely, as everyone knows, that apparently aberrant and meaningless phenomena—lapses, dreams, mental illness, etc.—become perfectly meaningful if one places them in a total structure embracing both the conscious and the unconscious of the individual whose development [*genèse*] one follows from birth.'[65]

[62] loc. cit.
[63] Goldmann, *Marxisme et sciences humaines*, p. 21.
[64] ibid., p. 27.   [65] ibid., p. 24.

Both Freud and Marx, he argues, have been the victims of positivistic misinterpretations:

'If Hegel, Marx and Freud represent in the history of the human sciences the major landmarks of a genetic structuralism which is both interpretative and explanatory, it is still true at the time when their works were produced the structuralist and interpretative side of their method was very little noticed even by them, still less by official science. The perspective of a non-interpretative causal explanation so dominated scientific thought that Marxism was seen as providing an explanation in terms of economic factors and psychoanalysis an explanation in terms of the libido.'[66]

Whether or not Goldmann is correct in identifying it with Marxism, this *verstehende* approach has been very influential and fruitful in the sociological analysis of culture and literature practised by Lukács, Goldmann and Mannheim. Lukács's concept of 'form', which he drew from his close friend Leo Popper[67] and which was anticipated by Simmel, is most prominent in his early pre-Marxist works.[68] As Peter Ludz emphasised, Lukács interpreted artistic products in terms of the relation between *forms of art* and *forms of life*.[69] In so doing, he could claim to be following Marx, who used the commodity form as his starting-point from which to lay bare 'all the objective forms of bourgeois society together with all the subjective forms corresponding to them'.[70]

The 'form' is interpolated in Lukács's explanations between the economic causes and their social and artistic consequences.[71] Thus, in the introduction to *Die Entwicklungsgeschichte des Modernen Dramas*, the connection which Lukács claims to be looking for is an indirect one:[72] 'The greatest error in the sociological treatment of art is that it looks for and investigates the content of artistic creations and tries to draw a straight line between this content and certain economic relations. But what is truly social in literature is the form.'[73]

Lukács uses the term 'form' in a number of ways. In his *Intro-*

[66] ibid., pp. 27f.

[67] See I. Mészáros, *Lukács' Concept of Dialectic* (London, Merlin, 1972), p. 120 and plate xv.

[68] Beginning with *Die Seele und die Formen* (Budapest, 1910, Berlin, 1911).

[69] Peter Ludz (ed.), Introduction to *G. Lukács: Schriften zur Literatursoziologie* (Neuwied, Luchterhand, 1961), p. 54.

[70] Lukács, *History and Class Consciousness*, p. 83.

[71] Ludz (ed.), op. cit., p. 7.

[72] ibid., p. 71 (cf. p. 55).

[73] Cf. Goldmann, *Marxisme et sciences humaines*, pp. 234f.

duction aux premiers écrits de G. Lukács,[74] Goldmann gives as examples of such forms those of the essay, tragedy, and romanticism in (*Soul and Form*), of the novel (in *The Theory of the Novel*) and of German philosophy and proletarian revolution (in *History and Class Consciousness*). Thus the novel-form, for instance, can be interpreted 'from above' in terms of the philosophy of history as 'the representative form of the age'.[75]

Mannheim, in a review of *The Theory of the Novel* strongly upheld the principle that interpretation must proceed 'from above'. What he calls a 'cultural phenomenon' (*geistiges Gebilde*) can be explained 'from below' (in psychological or sociological terms) only 'as a sociological phenomenon'; if, however, people

'claim an *exhaustive* explanation of the intellectual phenomenon in all its uniqueness, they are mistaken.

'Efforts to interpret objects, not "from below upward", but rather "from up downward", are quite a different matter. An example is the attempt at interpreting a form of art by an approach from metaphysics or philosophy of history. . . . The form is only an abstract component of the full spiritual content of the work of art and can be adequately abstracted from an aesthetic perspective. It follows that an interpretation of the abstract part is justified and possible only by proceeding from the whole.'[76]

The influence of the tradition we have been examining is most evident in Lukács's early works, *Soul and Form*, first published in 1910–1911, and *The Theory of the Novel* (1920). In his new preface of 1962 Lukács described the latter work as 'a typical product of *geisteswissenschaftlich* tendencies': the influence of Dilthey, Simmel and Weber had not yet been eclipsed, despite his 'passage from Kant to Hegel'. While emphasising the limits of this approach, and in particular the 'fashion to construct general synthetic concepts from what in most cases was a mere intuitive perception of a few tendencies peculiar to some movement or epoch' Lukács concedes 'its relative historical justification as against the pettiness and shallowness of neo-Kantian or other positivism'.[77]

Though Lukács retained the concept of 'form' in his later works, 'his turning to Marxism required a completely new account of the

---

[74] *Les Temps Modernes* (August 1962).
[75] G. Lukács, *The Theory of the Novel* (London, Merlin, 1971), p. 93.
[76] Kurt Wolff (ed.), *From Karl Mannheim* (New York, OUP, 1971), pp. 3ff.
[77] Lukács, *Theory of the Novel*, pp. 12f.

form-content relation. Lukács had to abandon the *a priori* character of the form.'[78] The question of the continuities and discontinuities in Lukács's work must be left to experts like Ludz, who suggests that his essential preoccupations remained relatively unchanged.[79] But whereas his early writings display a complex but identifiable methodological position, the threads are less easy to identify in his later work. It seems more useful to contrast his original position, with its stress on interpretation 'from above', with the attempts of both Goldmann and Mannheim to provide genetic explanations.

Goldmann's method in the sociology of literature consists essentially of identifying the 'meaningful structure' of the work to be investigated and understanding this structure as the expression of a world-view, a *Weltanschauung*. 'A work is philosophically, literally or aesthetically valid to the extent that it expresses a coherent view of the world in terms of concepts or verbal or sensory images, and one can understand and interpret it objectively only in so far as one succeeds in identifying the view which it expresses.'[80]

Earlier sociology of literature had been concerned 'with the content of literary works and the relationship between that content and the collective consciousness, that is to say, the ways in which men think and behave in daily life'.[81] It therefore emphasises the realistic 'reproduction of empirical reality and of daily life. In short, this sociology proves to be all the more fertile the more the works studied are mediocre. Moreover, what it seeks in these works is more documentary than literary in character.'[82] Genetic structuralist sociology, by contrast, assumes that:

> 'The essential relationship between the life of society and literary creation is not concerned with the content of these two sectors of human reality, but only with the mental structures, with what might be called the categories which shape both the empirical consciousness of a certain social group and the imaginary universe created by the writer.'[83]

Goldmann repeatedly emphasised the complementarity of understanding and explanation. Understanding (which is not a matter of

[78] Ludz, op. cit., p. 56. See also Lukács's essay '*Reportage oder Gestaltung*' (1932), Ludz, op. cit., p. 138.

[79] Ludz, op. cit., pp. 29ff. See also I. Mészáros, op. cit.

[80] L. Goldmann, *Recherches Dialectiques* (Paris, Gallimard, 1959), pp. 109ff.

[81] 'The Sociology of Literature', *International Social Science Journal* (1967), p. 494, Problems of Status and Method.

[82] loc. cit.

[83] ibid., p. 495.

empathy but 'a strictly intellectual process') 'consists in the description as precisely as possible of the significant structure' (of a work):

> 'Explanation is nothing other than the incorporation of this structure, as a constituent element, in an immediately embracing structure . . . in order to render intelligible the genesis of the work. . . . All that is necessary is to take the surrounding structure as an object of study and then what was explanation becomes comprehension and the explanatory research must be related to a new and even vaster structure. . . . To understand *Les Pensées* of Pascal or the tragedies of Racine is to bring to light the tragic vision which constitutes the significant structure governing the whole of each of these works; but to understand the structure of extremist Jansenism is to explain the genesis of *Les Pensées* and of the tragedies of Racine. Similarly, to understand Jansenism is to explain the genesis of extremist Jansenism; to understand the history of the *noblesse de robe* in the seventeenth century is to explain the genesis of Jansenism; to understand class relations in French society of the seventeenth century is to explain the evolution of the *noblesse de robe* etc.'[84]

On the previous page, he had expressed the distinction in the following terms:

> 'Comprehension is a problem of the inherent coherence of the text, which presupposes that the text, the whole text and nothing but the text is taken literally and that, within it, one seeks an overall significant structure. Explanation is a problem of seeking the individual or collective subject . . . in relation to which the mental structure which governs the work has a functional character and, for that very reason, a significant character.'[85]

This is still, then, an essentially interpretative method whose elements are, firstly, the structural homology between a work and the consciousness of a social group and, secondly, the concept of expression. At the level which Goldmann carved out for himself, it is enormously suggestive and interesting, but it clearly does not exhaust the possibilities of a sociology of literature. In particular, it has little to say about the mechanisms by which literary works are produced—not just their origin in the psychology of their producers but, more important from a sociological point of view, the 'real factors'[86] which further or inhibit intellectual production. For a treatment of these issues, we must turn to Mannheim's more broadly conceived sociology of knowledge and culture.

---

[84] ibid., p. 500.　　　　[85] ibid., p. 498.
[86] The term is Max Scheler's. See M. Scheler, *Die Wissensformen und die Gesellschaft* (*Werke*, Francke Verlag, Bern and Munich, 2nd edn, 1960), Vol. 8.

Karl Mannheim was not a Marxist, but he was very deeply influenced by Marxism. A contemporary of Lukács in the early years in Budapest, he collaborated with him and others in a lecture series in 1918.[87] There is no doubt that Mannheim owed a great deal to Lukács; Goldmann once wrote of Mannheim's sociology of knowledge that 'whatever is valuable in it was already present in Lukács's *Geschichte und Klassenbewusstsein*, which inspired it'.[88] There is, however, an essential difference between them. Two important strands came together in Lukács thought: firstly the *Geisteswissenschaft* tradition with its residual historicism, and secondly Marxism, considered as a form of ideological criticism which 'relativises' thought to its existential base. Both these currents had strong implications of relativism; Lukács considered that he had escaped this danger by identifying with the class position of the proletariat, which precisely because of its place in society, was able (at least in principle) to achieve an objective knowledge of social and historical reality which was denied to other classes and their intellectual representatives.[89] Without Lukács's Marxist belief, Mannheim wrestled throughout his life with the problem of relativism. His answers, such as they are, can be found in *Ideology and Utopia*; they centre around the notion of 'relationism' and, notoriously, the 'relatively classless' position of the 'free-floating intelligentsia'.[90]

The young Mannheim, as we have seen, enthusiastically upheld the view that a 'cultural object' could only be fully interpreted 'from above'. Gradually, though he came to take a more favourable view of the possibility of genetic sociological explanations of social phenomena which, by 1928, he was defending against dogmatic advocates of *Verstehen* such as Werner Sombart.[91] His early discussions of interpretation embody the central preoccupations of the *Geisteswissenschaft* tradition. In *Seele und Kultur*, for example, he discusses the relationship between a work and its creator. In one sense, he argues, the work is 'less than' its creator, since it refers back

[87] Mannheim's contribution, translated under the title '*Seele und Kultur*' is printed in Kurt Wolff, *Karl Mannheim: Wissenssoziologie* (Neuwied, Luchterhand, 1964).

[88] Goldmann, *Human Sciences and Philosophy*, p. 52.

[89] See the essays 'What is Orthodox Marxism?' and 'Class Consciousness' in *History and Class Consciousness* (esp. pp. 2f., 70–3). Lukács qualifies this position in his preface to the new German edition, written in 1967 (pp. xxiif. of the English translation).

[90] Karl Mannheim, *Ideology and Utopia* (London, Routledge, 1936).

[91] *Verhandlungen des 6 deutschen Soziologentages*, 1928.

to him: 'the thought means something and refers to the stream
of lived experience which it aims to fulfil. The ultimate meaning
of a creation escapes us if we lose our access to its subjective
origin.'[92]

But in another sense the work is more than the mind which
produces it, since it follows its own laws. Whereas the mind remains
chaotic and impenetrable for us, the material (*Stoff*) is formed into
a closed structure according to its particular laws. Thus, a poem, for
example, 'is subject to the laws of rhythm and literary genre'. In his
review of Lukács's *Theory of the Novel* the same distinction is drawn
in terms of different 'logical objects': a sociological explanation of a
cultural object explains it *qua* sociological structure. The work as a
whole can only be explained from above: 'This deeper mode of
explanation . . . we wish to call an *interpretation* in the narrower
sense of the word.'[93]

Mannheim further explicates his concept of interpretation in his
essay published in 1921–2 on 'The Interpretation of *Weltanschauung*'.[94] The human studies 'differ essentially from the natural
sciences when it comes to the relation of their respective logical
objects to the corresponding objects of prescientific, everyday experience'. The laws of physics 'can be expressed without reference to
the global content of . . . sensual experience . . . but for aesthetic
analysis . . . the object as given in pretheoretical, concrete experience
never ceases to be a problem'.[95]

Mannheim asks, then:

'What kind of task is a student of a cultural and historical discipline (a
historian of art, of religion, possibly also a sociologist) faced with when
he seeks to determine the *Weltanschauung* of an epoch, or to trace
partial manifestations back to this all-embracing entity? Is the entity
designated by the concept of *Weltanschauung* given to us at all, and if
so—*how* is it given? How does its givenness compare with that of other
data in the cultural and historical disciplines?'[96]

As he puts it later in the essay:[97] 'The crucial question is how the
totality we call the spirit, *Weltanschauung* of an epoch can be

---

[92] '*Seele und Kultur*', in Wolff (ed.), *Wissenssoziologie*, p. 71.
[93] ibid., pp. 87f.
[94] In *Essays on the Sociology of Knowledge*, Paul Kecskemeti (ed.) (London,
Routledge, 1952).
[95] ibid., p. 35.   [96] ibid., p. 33.
[97] ibid., p. 73.

distilled from the various "objectifications" of that epoch—and how
we can give a theoretical account of it.' In other words, the problem
is one of interpreting smaller-scale cultural phenomena *as* com-
ponents of a *Weltanschauung*.

Any cultural product, Mannheim argues, will display three
distinct strata of meaning: (*a*) its objective meaning; (*b*) its expressive
meaning; and (*c*) its documentary or evidential meaning. Objective
meaning is what is grasped by Weber's *'aktuelles Verstehen'*: the
basic identification of an action. Thus, when Mannheim's friend
gives a coin to a beggar the action is classified under some such
concept as 'assistance'. If the purpose of this act was to convey a
feeling of sympathy, this is the 'expressive meaning', the meaning
which was subjectively intended. 'Documentary meaning' is elicited
by a higher-order interpretation: 'That is, analysing all the implications of what I see, I may suddenly discover that the "act of charity"
was, in fact, one of hypocrisy.'[98] We can, Mannheim points out,

> 'on occasion apply this last mode of interpretation to *ourselves* as well.
> The expressive-intentional interpretation of our own objectifications is
> no problem for us. The expressive meaning we intended to convey in any
> one of our acts was immediately given in the living context and we can
> always bring it back to consciousness (except, of course, in cases where
> memory fails us). But the documentary significance of an action of ours
> is quite another matter and may be as much of a problem for us as if
> in our own objectifications we were brought face to face with a total
> stranger. Hardly anywhere is there such a sharp contrast between the
> expressive and documentary interpretation as in this borderline case of
> "self-recognition". And the totality we call the "genius" or the "spirit"
> (of an epoch) is given to us in this mode of "documentary meaning";
> this is the perspective in which we grasp the elements that go to make
> up the global outlook of a creative individual or of an epoch.'[99]

The documentary meaning of a cultural phenomenon, or at least
part of that meaning, is given by its place in a larger structure such
as a *Weltanschauung*. Mannheim raises, but does not attempt to
answer, the question of how one should characterise the relationships
between these phenomena:

> 'whether the unity of various cultural fields should be expressed in terms
> of "correspondence", "function", "causality" or "reciprocity". . . . The
> historian may have isolated with complete certainty one and the same
> "documentary" symptom in several cultural domains; still, the question

[98] ibid., p. 47.
[99] ibid., p. 48.

which form of connection should be interpolated will have to be solved separately. The category of causality—which largely governs the explanations of natural science—seems to be best suited for this task. But—even apart from the question what "causal explanation" means in the cultural sciences and what its scope is—we may very well ask whether tracing a phenomenon back, not to another phenomenon, but to a "global outlook" behind both, does not constitute a type of explanation which is totally different from genetic, historical, causal explanation. If the term "explanation" is to be reserved for the latter, we propose to call the former "interpretation" [*Deutung*].'[100]

There seems to be a systematic ambiguity in the essay as to whether what is at issue is the interpretation of *Weltanschauungen* as such or the interpretation of other cultural phenomena in terms of *Weltanschauungen*. In fact, of course, the two are related in the 'hermeneutic circle': 'We understand the whole from the part, and the part from the whole. We derive the "spirit of the epoch" from its individual documentary manifestations—and we interpret the individual documentary manifestations on the basis of what we know about the spirit of the epoch.'[101] What criteria then apply to documentary interpretations? Mannheim claims that 'cultural products which we consider from the documentary point of view always unmistakably impose or exclude certain interpretations'.[102] But this is hardly satisfactory; ultimately the only test of a documentary interpretation which he can suggest is the formal one that it 'must cover the total range of the cultural manifestations of an epoch'.[103] Mannheim concludes:

'Interpretation does not make causal explanation superfluous. It refers to something quite different, and consequently there is absolutely no rivalry between the two. Interpretation serves for the deeper understanding of meanings; causal explanation shows the conditions for the actualisation or realisation of a given meaning. . . . Understanding is the adequate grasping of an intended meaning or of the validity of a preposition (this, then, includes the objective as well as the expressive stratum of meaning); interpretation means bringing the abstractively distinguished strata of meaning in correlation to each other and especially to the documentary stratum. In the history of art, and in the cultural sciences in general, the procedures we have so sharply distinguished—causal explanation and interpretation—will, of course, both be applied *in turn* (but not in the same breath!) in order to give as good an idea as possible of the full, concrete variety and "vitality" of the

[100] ibid., pp. 80f.   [101] ibid., p. 74.
[102] ibid., p. 62.   [103] loc. cit.

historical process in question—although it is also quite rewarding to analyse an epoch consistently from a purely interpretative viewpoint.'[104]

The essay on *Weltanschauungen* is Mannheim's most systematic account in his early writings of the relationship between interpretation (which as we have seen includes 'understanding') on the one hand, and causal explanation on the other. It should be compared with a later essay on the 'Ideological and Sociological Interpretation of Intellectual Phenomena'.[105]

By this time (1926) Mannheim had published the 'Structural Analysis of Epistemology'[106] which he had mentioned in *Seele und Kultur*; a long essay on 'Historicism';[107] and his first treatment of the 'sociology of knowledge',[108] *'Das Problem einer Soziologie des Wissens'*. 'Sociological interpretation' now means something very different to Mannheim from what he understood by it in his review of *The Theory of the Novel*; it now involves the bringing together of 'the entire ideological sphere with the social reality underlying it and is as such the highest stage of any total interpretation'.[109]

In the course of the article Mannheim works his way slowly towards the typology printed at the end. Ideas, he says, can either be studied from inside as 'ideas' (*Innenbetrachtung*) or from the outside as 'ideologies' (*Aussenbetrachtung*). The latter process involves the 'relativisation' of the idea to another sphere of reality by demonstrating its 'function'. This external approach may be either idealistic or positivistic in character: sociological interpretations are a subclass of positivistic interpretations; the factors which make up their system of reference are primarily economic and social, whereas other positivistic interpretations may have recourse to biological or other factors. An external approach to an idea, whether it is incorporated in a literary work or a theoretical system affords a 'new method of interpretation' and adds to our understanding of that idea.

These are really interpretations (rather than purely causal explana-

[104] ibid., p. 81.

[105] 'The Ideological and Sociological Interpretation of Intellectual Phenomena', in Wolff (ed.), *From Karl Mannheim*.

[106] In *Essays on Sociology and Social Psychology*, Paul Kecskemeti (ed.) (London, Routledge, 1953).

[107] 'Historicism', in Kecskemeti (ed.), *Essays on the Sociology of Knowledge*, pp. 84–133.

[108] 'The Problem of a Sociology of Knowledge', ibid., pp. 134–90.

[109] 'The Ideological and Sociological Interpretation of Intellectual Phenomena', in Wolff (ed.), *From Karl Mannheim*, pp. 129f.

tions of the sort provided by explanatory psychology) since what they elicit are not purely causal preconditions (*Vorbedingungen*) but 'presuppositions' in terms of meaning (*Voraussetzungen*). The 'social being' to which they refer is a meaningful whole (*Sinnzusammenhang*):

> 'When Marx for instance tries *to explain* the explanatory method of the eighteenth century which always starts from the individual . . . in terms of the nature of a bourgeois society of free competition, this is *not* an explanation of a theoretical axiomatic system in terms of non-meaningful reality [*aus sinnfremdem Sein*] but rather an interpretation of this ultimate theoretical system of a historical type of thought in terms of a more comprehensive order of existence which underlies it and which is *grasped as meaningful.*'[110]

What Mannheim thought a sociological interpretation should look like can be seen from his other writings of the period, the essays on 'Conservative Thought'[111] and on 'The Problem of Generations'[112] and, most ambitiously in *Ideology and Utopia*[113] and in 'Competition as a Cultural Phenomenon'.[114] In the last of these, Mannheim is concerned with the question whether what he calls, following Heidegger, the 'public interpretation of reality' comes about:

1. on the basis of a *consensus of opinion*, of spontaneous co-operation between individuals and groups;
2. on the basis of the *monopoly-position* of one particular group;
3. on the basis of competition between many groups, each determined to impose on others their particular interpretation of the world (*atomistic competition*);
4. on the basis of a *concentration* round one point of view of a number of formerly atomistically competing groups, as a result of which competition as a whole is gradually concentrated around a few poles which become more and more dominant.[115]

The first two types, he argues, both rely on a high degree of social stability; this restricts the 'range of sensitivity' of thought within the society. This stability may be the result of homogeneity, as in the first case, or of the monopoly of a particular group such as the medieval Church or the Chinese *literati*. The breakdown of this

---

110 ibid., p. 122.   111 ibid., p. 123.
112 Both in Kecskemeti (ed.), *Essays on Sociology and Social Psychology*.
113 Mannheim, *Ideology and Utopia*.
114 Kecskemeti (ed.), *Essays on the Sociology of Knowledge*.
115 ibid., pp. 198f.

monopoly gives rise to 'atomistic competition' by mutually hostile groups and finally, in the fourth case which Mannheim discusses, these groups and their world-views may reform in broader coalitions; the example he gives is of the gradual coalescence of European conservative thought in response to the growth of liberalism.

The 'inner structure' of a world-view, its 'range of sensitivity', will depend on its 'sociologically determined genesis' defined in terms of the four 'pure types' above. Thus 'any expert will be able to indicate, on the basis of a simple inspection of any given world conception or thought pattern, whether it has come into being as a result of atomistic competition between individual groups, on the basis of a consensus, or of a monopoly of a dominating group'.[116]

I have tried to show, at least in outline, what Mannheim meant by 'interpretation'; his conception, despite its sketchy presentation and the weakness of its philosophical foundations, remains one of the most fruitful available to the sociologist. It suggests, in the sociology of knowledge and culture at least, a possible middle way between the crudities of a positivist or vulgar-Marxist approach and the circularity of a purely interpretative one. In the final paragraph of 'Competition', Mannheim justified the method which he followed throughout his mature work:

> 'This does not mean to say that the mind and thought are nothing but the expression and reflex of various "locations" in the social fabric, and that there exist only quantitatively determinable functional correlations and no potentiality of "freedom" grounded in mind; it merely means that even within the sphere of the intellectual, there are processes amenable to rational analysis, and that it would be an ill-advised mysticism which would shroud things in romantic obscurity at a point where rational cognition is still practicable. Anyone who wants to drag in the irrational where the lucidity and acuity of reason still must rule by right merely shows that he is afraid to face the mystery at its legitimate place.'[117]

In the discussion which followed his original presentation of the paper at the Sixth Congress of German Sociologists he returned to this theme, and drew an important and timely political conclusion. Mannheim argued, against the claims both of 'idealism' and of 'materialism', that while *some* cultural phenomena cannot be explained mechanically, other *can* be so explained:

[116] loc. cit.
[117] ibid., pp. 228f.

'It is very curious that this mechanistic approach which is so much despised permits an accurate and virtually complete explanation of certain movements and very important phenomena in our contemporary situation. So why should one not make use of it? . . . I consider it a terrible danger in German thought (and this danger is only the other side of one of its finest qualities) that its interpretative tendency leads it to try to interpret what can only be explained. Having discovered the tremendous depth and unique quality of the phenomenon of understanding (*Verstehen*), it also tries to "deepen" and to make into a question of interpretation what can only be adequately grasped in terms of the concepts of "doing", of "mechanism". This methodological error of interpreting what one ought to explain is merely a methodological expression of an unpolitical attitude of mind which has often enough been observed in life itself.'[118]

Mannheim's speech to the German sociologists brings us back to the questions raised at the beginning of this chapter. As a criticism of German intellectual life it seems fully justified, but I shall argue later in this book, mainly in the concluding chapter, that a *verstehende* approach is not necessarily only contemplative and practically impotent. It seems quite compatible with a *verstehende* orientation to make available to the people one is studying a range of alternative concepts which they may find useful in understanding their own situation and lead them to see it in a new light. It is not difficult to imagine circumstances in which such a 'transformation of consciousness' might have dramatic practical consequences.

[118] *Verhandlungen des 6 deutschen Soziologentages*, p. 122.

F

6

Meaning and Subjectivity

The claim that social phenomena and, in particular, social action are 'meaningful', tends to be made as though it were self-explanatory. The term has been so loosely used that one adds to this discussion only with considerable trepidation. Part of the problem is the absence of a satisfactory account even of linguistic meaning which could serve as a point of reference for the extended (or perhaps even metaphorical) use of the concept by social science. Problems of semantics were, for a long time, virtually excluded from linguistics, on the grounds that they were not amenable to scientific investigation. The formalists upheld a methodological scepticism which 'neither says that meaning does not exist nor that linguistic forms have no meaning; it states no more than that, since meaning is an elusive thing, linguistics should ignore it and work only on external descriptions of languages and linguistic behaviour'.[1] 'Generative semantics', which attempts to repeat Chomsky's achievement in generative syntax, remains programmatic.[2] An alternative approach to meaning, based to some extent on Wittgenstein's later work, has so far been largely confined to analytic philosophy of language.[3]

There is, however, a reasonably clear division of opinion which is lucidly characterised by Strawson in his inaugural lecture of 1969:

'For the sake of label, we might call it the conflict between the theorists of communication-intention and the theorists of formal semantics.

[1] Tullio de Mauro, *Ludwig Wittgenstein: His Place in the Development of Semantics* (The Hague, Martinus Nijhoff, 1967), p. 37.

[2] John Searle, 'Chomsky's Revolution in Linguistics', *New York Review of Books* (29 June 1972), p. 20.

[3] See, for instance, Searle's *Speech Acts* (Cambridge University Press, 1969) and J. R. Searle (ed.), *The Philosophy of Language* (Oxford University Press, 1971).

According to the former, it is impossible to give an adequate account of the concept of meaning without reference to the possession by speakers of audience directed intentions of a certain complex kind. The particular meanings of words and sentences are, no doubt, largely a matter of rule and convention; but the general nature of such rules and conventions can be ultimately understood only by reference to the concept of communication-intention. The opposed view, at least in its negative aspect, is that this doctrine simply gets things the wrong way round or the wrong way up, or mistakes the contingent for the essential. Of course we may expect a certain regularity of relationship between what people intend to communicate by uttering certain sentences and what those sentences conventionally mean. But the system of semantic and syntactical rules, in the mastery of which knowledge of a language consists—the rules which determine the meanings of sentences—is not a system of rules *for* communicating at all. The rules can be exploited for this purpose; but this is incidental to their essential character. . . .'[4]

One can see certain similarities in the different ways social scientists treat the 'meaning' of social phenomena. Schutz discusses the meaning of actions phenomenologically in terms of intentional acts of *Sinngebung*, while a more 'formal' approach is represented by tendencies such as functionalism, systems theory and modern French structuralism (in which the linguistic analogy is most explicit). The area of disagreement could be summarised very roughly in the following terms: an action is 'meaningful' (*a*) in virtue of an intentional act of the agent, which may occur in his retrospective grasp of his action or in the 'project' which preceded it; or (*b*) in virtue of the 'system' to which it belongs. For Dilthey, this was merely the wider context (e.g. the whole of the agent's life). More plausibly, it could be the system of action-guiding norms (Parsons), or action-constituting rules (Winch), or a complex system which is external to the consciousness of the agents but which is sustained by their actions (in different ways, Lévi-Strauss, Parsons, etc.).

It should not be assumed that (*a*) and (*b*) are mutually exclusive, nor that they are jointly exhaustive of some reified concept of 'meaning'. What we are trying to identify (and it is every bit as elusive as linguistic meaning) is what it is that distinguishes human actions from the movements of physical bodies and the behaviour of

[4] P. F. Strawson, *Meaning and Truth* (Oxford University Press, 1970), pp. 4f. In the article cited above, Searle quotes Chomsky to the effect that 'meaning need not involve communication or even the attempt to communicate' (Searle, *New York Review of Books*, p. 23).

animals. Perhaps the least misleading way to express this distinction is to say that human action is 'intentional'.[5]

The way in which social scientists deal with these considerations, the balance in their methodologies between understanding and causal explanation, allows one to place them on a rough continuum between extreme behaviourism and the view that human actions are fundamentally refractory to causal explanation. Weber's brilliant synthesis was unstable in two respects. Although he resolved, programmatically at least, the problem of combining *Motivationsverstehen* with causal explanation,[6] he neglected the problems of both direct understanding (*aktuelles Verstehen*) and the understanding of 'meaningful structures' (*Sinngebilde*). Weber is thus the point of reference for more recent approaches to these problems.

One possible response to the problems of a *verstehende* sociology is to reject this approach entirely in favour of some form of behaviourism which claims that the social scientist can manage without *verstehende* access to his data. The success of ethology is alleged to show, as Habermas puts it, that 'purposive adaptive behaviour can be grasped and analysed without reference to intentions' and that the latter can be reduced to behavioural dispositions. 'Intentional action need not be denied, but it is enough to investigate the observable behaviour in which it manifests itself.'[7]

I cannot attempt to show here that behaviourist accounts of social phenomena are necessarily impoverished, nor to argue, as Habermas does, that they presuppose a behaviourist account of language which has been devastatingly criticised by Chomsky in his review of Skinner's 'verbal behaviour'.[8] It can, however, be argued that

[5] Part of the appeal of putting it this way may be the possibility of equivocation between the linguistic notion of intentionality (as applied to statements, beliefs, etc. that something is the case) and the more restricted psychological notion of intention. Wittgenstein, for example, showed that we are prepared to impute beliefs, hopes, fears, etc. to animals only within certain limits: 'A dog believes his master is at the door. But can he also believe his master will come the day after tomorrow? . . . Can only those hope who can talk? Only those who have mastered the use of a language?' (L. Wittgenstein, *Philosophical Investigations*, translated by E. Anscombe and R. Rhees (Oxford University Press, 1953), p. 174e).

[6] There is a practical illustration in the industrial inquiry which he undertook for the *Verein* into the determinants of workers' output (*Gesammelte Aufsätze zur Soziologie und Sozialpolitik* (Tübingen, Mohr, 1924), pp. 131ff.).

[7] J. Habermas, *Zur Logik der Sozialwissenschaften* (Frankfurt, Suhrkamp, 1970), p. 147.

[8] N. Chomsky, Review of B. F. Skinner's *Verbal Behaviour*, in *Language*, Vol. 35 (1959); reprinted in J. A. Fodor and J. J. Katz (eds), *The Structure of*

behaviourism in fact depends on the existence of intentional relations:

'The class of observable events which we call "behaviour" is distinguished from the class of other events by a system of reference which makes explicit an understandable connection. This system of reference constitutes a functional relation between the original state of an organism, its environment (including conditions of existence and stimuli) and its final state; these quantities are connected by an observable behavioural reaction. The relation is functionalist in terms of need-satisfaction, and this is not directly observable. We understand in advance what it is to satisfy a need; we should never come to understand it through observation alone. . . .'[9]

'It is precisely the unacknowledged but unbreakable attachment of the behaviourist approach to a linguistically articulated preunderstanding [*Vorverständnis*] of experience in the everyday world of social life which explains why behaviourist theories of human behaviour are possible. Language cannot be reduced to behaviour, but if we presuppose an initial understanding through linguistic communication of the hidden intentionality of behaviour we can analyse intentional action behaviouristically.'[10]

It is in this context that one can understand Abel's account of *Verstehen* as the (hypothetical) interpolation of a 'behaviour maxim' between two observed events.[11] In Abel's first example a man lights a fire after a sudden drop in temperature, and the connection seems obvious enough; it can be described as the response of an organism to a change in its environment. But the use of a form of stimulus-response language to describe the behaviour of farmers who postpone their impending marriages in the face of a bad harvest is less convincing; the 'behaviour maxim' is no longer trivial. In an 'alien' culture in which neither an S-R schema nor, at the extreme, the schema of instrumental rationality apparently clarified the situation, Abel's observer would be at a loss. In other words, the 'maxims' are not so much given by introspection or 'self-evident' as underwritten by the language and practices of a community.

The existence of this 'stock of knowledge' embodied in everyday

Language: Readings in the Philosophy of Language (Hemel Hempstead, Prentice-Hall, 1964).

[9] Habermas, op. cit., p. 162.

[10] ibid., p. 164.

[11] Theodore Abel, 'The Operation Called *Verstehen*', *American Journal of Sociology* (1958).

life and ordinary language is emphasised by Cicourel and by Harré and Secord. As they see it, it casts considerable doubt on the desirability of 'operationalising' concepts in social science, or at least suggests that most operationalisations have been over-hasty and conceptually crude:

> 'operations can never be a *substitute* for the concepts to which they are related. They can relate to them only in some specified fashion that leaves the one conceptually independent of the other. Operations may define the measure of a certain property, or they may identify the effect of a certain cause and action. Clear accounts of the concepts themselves are needed, along with precise statements of the relation of the properties and states described by such concepts as dissonance to the phenomena which can be observed, and which "operations" are designed to measure.'[12]

This is not a romantic protest that conceptualisation fails to capture the 'soul of things'; it objects to the replacement of the relatively precise concepts of everyday language by operational concepts which though 'measurable', are imprecise.

> 'What are the appropriate foundations for measurement in sociology? The literature discussed above implies that with our present state of knowledge rigorous measurement (in the literal sense which obtains with the use of explicit theoretical systems) cannot be obtained in sociology for the properties of social process. The precise measurement of social process requires first the study of the problem of meaning in everyday life.'[13]

If one rejects the behaviourist reduction of intentional action to stimulated behaviour there is an alternative approach to a general theory in the so-called 'theory of action', which discusses action in relation to institutionalised values and norms, and tends towards a functionalist and systems-theoretical scheme of interpretation. It would be unwise to generalise from the single example of Parsons and to assert that a theory of action *must* emphasise its normative

[12] R. Harré and P. F. Secord, *The Explanation of Social Behaviour* (Oxford, Blackwell, 1972), pp. 36f. Cf. ibid., p. 133, 'It is one of the major contentions of this book that, while the statistical method is, with certain reservations and safeguards, a reasonable way of trying to discover and extend the critical description of social behaviour, it is impossible to use it as a method for discovering the generative mechanisms at work in social life.'

[13] A. V. Cicourel, *Method and Measurement in Sociology* (Glencoe, Free Press, 1964), pp. 14f. The essentially phenomenological analysis of the 'world of everyday life' which Cicourel advocates is not without its difficulties (see below, pp. 92f.)

conditioning;[14] nor does Parsons's transition from a normative theory of action to a functionalist analysis of the 'social system' seem logically necessary.[15] It seems, nevertheless, fairly clear that if the purpose of a normative theory of action is to 'permit assumptions about the empirical system [*Zusammenhang*] of valid norms'[16] functionalism makes it possible to grasp this objective system as a meaningful one. 'This system transcends the subjectively intended meaning of those who act according to norms, but as an empirical system of norms it shares their meaningful aspect. The system is not intended by the acting subjects but is nevertheless intentional.'[17]

But as positivist critics of functionalism in social science have repeatedly shown, the system it postulates and the limits of tolerance of that system cannot be empirically specified; the method cannot claim to provide empirical knowledge but 'functions' merely as a normative scheme of possible heuristic value.[18] Parsons makes the

[14] Parsons does not make this claim, though he does argue that such an approach is superior to utilitarian or other 'positivistic' theories of action. (T. Parsons, *The Structure of Social Action* (Glencoe, Free Press, 2nd edn, 1949,) pp. 74–82.

[15] Harold Bershady, in his book *Ideology and Social Knowledge* (Oxford, Blackwell, 1973) suggests why Parsons's thought took this course, and also emphasises the continuity of his theoretical preoccupations. Cf. Alain Touraine's claim that the 'transition of action analysis into functionalist analysis cannot be defined in general terms, and its character changes according to the theme and the level under consideration'. (A. Touraine, 'Towards a Sociology of Action', reprinted in A. Giddens (ed.), *Positivism and Sociology* (London, Heinemann, 1974), pp. 86f. Touraine's work is briefly discussed below (note 23).)

[16] Habermas, op. cit., p. 166.

[17] loc. cit.

[18] Bershady (op. cit.) emphasises the *a priori* nature of Parsons's approach and considers his use of 'necessary reasoning', 'the single most pervasive feature of his work' (p. 146). The set of features held to be necessary is extended as Parsons's thought develops.

'First, the categories of the means-end framework were proposed as logically necessary for all social thought. Then, each of the functional subsystems was conceived to be necessary to any social system. To all of this was added the conditions of structural and temporal differentiation of the units of any social system held to be necessary for the existence of the system. Following, there was proposed the "hierarchy of cybernetic control" as an ingredient apparently necessary (though vaguely stated) to organise the subsystems of any societal systems. And presently—although we have no idea whether this will be the end of it all—the modalities of society are not merely logically construed combinations of the elements, but are conceived to occur in a necessary temporal sequence: certain variations of society cannot occur before the others.' (pp. 148f.)

transition 'from the analysis of the structure of social action as such to the structural-functional analysis of social systems';[19] or as W. L. Wallace puts it, from 'social actionism' which emphasises 'the social generation and maintenance of subjective dispositions in role incumbents' to 'functional imperativism' which makes imposed imperatives of the social system the explanatory concepts.[20] 'Thus what Parsons suggested with an empirical-analytic purpose turns into a "systems theory" which investigates the functioning of a social institution in terms of a pragmatically presupposed system-goal.'[21]

Although functionalism cannot be vindicated as a general theory of social systems, it may serve, as Habermas suggests, as a useful interpretative scheme for historically directed social analysis.[22] This question, however, lies outside the scope of the present study; from this point of view functionalism can best be understood as a possible mode of *interpretation* which grasps relations which, although not present in the minds of social agents, can be described, if only metaphorically, in teleological terms and hence understood as 'meaningful'.[23] Max Weber seems to have taken something like this view of functional interpretation, which he conceived as a preliminary to the proper tasks of sociology:

'How far in other disciplines this type of functional analysis of the relation of "parts" to a "whole" can be regarded as definitive, cannot be

[19] T. Parsons, op. cit., preface to second edition.
[20] W. L. Wallace, *Sociological Theory* (London, Heinemann, 1969).
[21] Habermas, op. cit., p. 178. Cf. Wallace, op. cit., p. 39.
[22] ibid., pp. 179, 305–8.
[23] Cf. Bershady, op. cit., Chapter 8. Alain Touraine's non-functionalist 'action sociology', as expressed in his *Sociologie de l'Action* (Paris, Seuil, 1965) and in two papers which are now available in English in Giddens (ed.), *Positivism and Sociology*, attempts to provide an interpretation of this sort in terms of the 'historical subject'.
This concept is extremely unclear in Touraine's work. It is not, he emphasises, to be identified with either the individual or society, nor with the 'spirit' of a culture (Touraine, op. cit., p. 120). Giddens writes in his introduction (p. 16) to *Positivism and Sociology*: 'The historical subject does not have a fixed empirical referent and is most aptly understood as a methodological principle for understanding the *unité totalisante* of social action as a creator of meaning.'
Touraine seems to be aiming at a *verstehende* analysis of social action which is not cast in terms of established values and norms but includes a historical account of the origin of those values. He stops short of the transition to functionalist analysis, which he considers complementary to action theory but logically posterior to it ('Toward a Sociology of Action', in Giddens (ed.), op. cit., especially pp. 86ff.).

discussed here; but it is well known that the biochemical and biological modes of analysis of the organism are on principle opposed to stopping there. For purposes of sociological analysis two things can be said. Firstly, this functional frame of reference is convenient for purposes of practical illustration and for provisional orientation. But at the same time if its cognitive value is overestimated and its concept illegitimately "reified" it can be highly dangerous. Secondly, in certain circumstances this is the only available way of determining just what processes of social action it is important to understand in order to explain a given phenomenon. But this is only the beginning of sociological analysis as here understood.'[24]

Karl Mannheim sometimes hints at a bolder approach when he discusses 'objective meanings' in terms of the concept of function, though it should be noted that he uses this term less frequently and less consistently than 'structure'. Functional language is most clearly in evidence in a long essay, written in the early thirties, but not published until 1956, 'Towards the Sociology of the Mind'.[25]

In a section entitled 'The Proper and Improper Concept of Mind', Mannheim attempts to purge Hegel's concept of 'objective mind' of its speculative elements. What he retains, essentially, is the notion that 'mental phenomena have a structure and a supra-individual dimension'.[26] 'The strength of the Hegelian *Geist* concept lies . . . in its grasp of the social dimensions of meaning, and it is this fact which makes the distinction between the subjective act and its objective counterpart, the socially relevant meaning, possible.'[27]

'The question, raised even by Max Weber, of how we move from individual experiences to an objective meaning or to the sociological point of view, is a topsy-turvy version of the real question of how we get from the concrete social meaning of things to Max Weber's individually intended meaning or to the conception of an abstract sphere of detached significations[28] . . . Max Weber's oversimplified conception of the "meaning" of an action—as an intended or unconscious aim—prevented him from realising the objective or functional meaning of behaviour.'[29]

[24] Weber, *Economy and Society* (New York, Bedminster, 1968), p. 15.
[25] In Karl Mannheim, *Essays on the Sociology of Culture*, edited by Ernest Manheim (London, Routledge, 1956).
[26] ibid., p. 69.   [27] ibid., p. 68.
[28] ibid., p. 66.   [29] ibid., p. 77.

Mannheim argues that '*what* constitutes a historical or social fact can only be understood through its function'.[30] The example he gives is the family which, he claims, is defined primarily by its child-rearing function. This *interpretation* in functional terms does not rule out, though it seems to be prior to, *causal* explanations in terms of the 'impulses which are at work in the formation of families: the quest for companionship, security, sex and economic considerations'.[31]

'In the causal view we seek to *construe* an event through as many of its determinants as we are able to isolate. The final construct is largely an approximation of the actual event, and when the approximation is close enough for a given purpose we say the event is *explained*. On the other hand, we *interpret* the same occurrence if we detect its function in the equilibrium of the whole system in which it takes place. The conception of the system as an equilibrium is merely a heuristic device and is equally applicable to changing as well as to static structures. The function of an event is its necessary role in a system or, more specifically, it is the particular manner in which the heuristically assumed equilibrium of the system is conditioned by that event.'[32]

This account of the place of functional analysis is not worked out in detail, but it seems fair to say that the linguistic similarities with the work of more recent functionalists conceal important differences of approach. As T. Z. Lavine has shown, the structure or system to which Mannheim's concept of function corresponds is 'a spiritual [*geistige*] rather than a biological model of organic unity'.[33] On the other hand, it might be argued, on the lines suggested above and in Bershady's interpretation of Parsons, that while contemporary functionalism may have begun with the use of suspect biological analogies and the aspiration to construct a 'general theory of society', the real contribution of such analyses can more plausibly be seen as some sort of interpretation.

Functionalism attempts to come to grips with the 'objective meanings' of social phenomena by treating them as parts of an intentional complex, but this is ultimately unsuccessful; the meanings or 'functions' are not discovered empirically but laid down in

[30] loc. cit.
[31] loc. cit.
[32] ibid., p. 76.
[33] Thelma Z. Lavine, 'Karl Mannheim and Contemporary Functionalism', *Philosophy and Phenomenological Research*, Vol. 25, No. 4 (1965); reprinted in Gunter Remmling (ed.), *Towards the Sociology of Knowledge* (London, Routledge, 1973).

advance. The problem of *Verstehen* is circumscribed, but at the cost of the theory's empirical character.[34] Phenomenological approaches to this problem, despite their heterogeneity, have a common theme in the attempt to reconstruct the genesis of these objective meanings in the intersubjective communication of individuals in the 'social life-world'.

The reference to Weber is clearest in Alfred Schutz's major work, *The Phenomenology of the Social World*.[35] According to Schutz, Weber 'naïvely took for granted the meaningful phenomena of the social world as a matter of *intersubjective agreement* in precisely the same way as we all in daily life assume the existence of a lawful external world conforming to the concepts of our understanding . . .'. But 'far from being homogeneous, the social world is given to us in a complex system of perspectives. . . . Here we are not referring to differences between the personal standpoints from which different people look at the world but to the fundamental differences between my interpretation of my own subjective experiences (self-interpretation) and my interpretation of the subjective experiences of someone else.'[36]

Objective social science can have no other basis than 'the already constituted meanings of active participants in the social world',[37] but it cannot remain at the subjective level of these meanings. Hence 'the theme of all the sciences of the social world is to constitute an objective meaning-context either out of subjective meaning-contexts generally or out of some particular subjective meaning-contexts. The problem of every social science can, therefore, be summarised in the question: How are sciences of subjective meaning-context possible?'[38] In other words, how is Weber possible?

Schutz correctly realises that it is the ideal type which must mediate this transition from the subjective to the objective if anything can. When we construct an ideal type, whether purely of a person's character or of a course of action, we are not thinking of the particular experience or characteristics of the individual in question, but

[34] Habermas, op. cit., pp. 184f. In Habermas's terms, the theory becomes 'normative-analytic', yielding hypothetical imperatives for the 'system' which resemble those imposed on agents in, for example, decision theory.
[35] Alfred Schutz, *The Phenomenology of the Social World* (London, Heinemann, 1972). Translation of *Der Sinnhafte Aufbau der sozialen Welt. Eine Einleitung in die verstehende Soziologie* (Vienna, Springer, 1932).
[36] ibid., pp. 8f.   [37] ibid., p. 10.
[38] ibid., p. 223.

rather of giving an interpretation in terms of typical patterns of events which could occur 'again and again' in the lives of different individuals. 'The subjective meaning-context has been abandoned as a tool of interpretation. It has been replaced by a series of highly complex and systematically interrelated objective meaning-contexts.'[39] But these interpretations in terms of ideal-types are only 'probable'[40] and Schutz seems to mean by 'objectivity' no more than that they are 'subject to constant adjustment and revision on the basis of the observer's experience' and that they make up our 'stock of knowledge at hand'.[41]

This is not, I think, merely a verbal point. The root of the problem lies in Schutz's phenomenological concept of meaning which is radically individualistic and subjective.[42] Meaning is reduced to the *act* of *Sinngebung* or *Sinnsetzung*; it 'is merely an operation of intentionality'.[43] It was his emphasis on this aspect of meaning, as much as his essentially Cartesian epistemology, which pushed Husserl towards a solipsistic position from which he tried to extricate himself in his later writings by introducing the concept of the '*Lebenswelt*'.[44] Schutz impressively anticipates much of Husserl's later work, but neither can ultimately escape from the subjectivistic starting-point. Habermas has characterised the phenomenological approach in a splendid metaphor: 'The monads spin linguistic intersubjectivity out of their own resources [*erst aus sich heraus*]. Language is not yet grasped as the web on whose threads the subjects hang and on which they first begin to make themselves into subjects.'[45]

Like Schutz, modern phenomenological sociologists such as Harold Garfinkel and Aaron Cicourel attempt a *verstehende* analysis of the 'world of everyday life' and in particular of actors' 'definitions' of their situation. 'Patterns of responses may enable us to infer the existence and substantive properties of norms, but these patterns do not tell us how the actor perceives the role of the other and then shapes his self-role accordingly.'[46] The emphasis on problems of

[39] ibid., p. 184.   [40] ibid., p. 193.

[41] loc. cit.

[42] ibid., Ch. 2: 'The Constitution of Meaningful Lived Experience in the Constitutor's Own Stream of Consciousness.'

[43] ibid., p. 52.

[44] Cf. Edo Pivčević, *Husserl and Phenomenology* (London, Hutchinson, 1970), Ch. 8.

[45] Habermas, op. cit., p. 220.

[46] Cicourel, op. cit., pp. 202f.

'meaning' and 'social definition' generates, as I suggested above, a powerful critique of premature 'operationalisation' and conceptual 'reification'. Cicourel writes:

> 'Anyone engaged in field research will find that the shorthand vocabulary of social science is very similar to the general norms stated in some penal code: they do not correspond to explicit sequences of events and social meanings, but the fit is "managed" through negotiated socially organised activities of the police, prosecution, witnesses, the judge and the suspect or defendant. . . .'[47]

Though such a position may lead ultimately to an extreme empiricism which denies the possibility of rational knowledge[48] it seems likely that social scientists might benefit from paying closer attention to the 'prescientific' ways of interpreting and explaining social action which are embodied in everyday life.[49]

But there seems to be, in much recent work of this genre, a more radical and less plausible claim that the analysis of patterns of communicative behaviour in the world of everyday life, by means of socio-linguistic studies or the experiments to which Harold Garfinkel has given his name,[50] will lay bare a structure of 'basic rules of everyday life' underlying the more or less visible 'rules of conduct'. This suggests, as Dreitzel[51] and others have pointed out, that a 'phenomenological sociology' is committed to some sort of transcendental investigation which could take as its starting-point either the transcendental ego of classical phenomenology or the analysis of

[47] ibid., p. 13.

[48] Barry Hindess, *The Use of Official Statistics in Sociology. A Critique of Positivism and Ethnomethodology* (London, Macmillan, 1973), p. 26.

[49] This view is strongly argued by Harré and Secord (op. cit.). They suggest that the relatively precise concepts of everyday language, refined by philosophical analysis, afford a better way of explaining social behaviour than the reified concepts of positivist sociology and social psychology. Moreover, they claim, such explanations resemble those of the advanced (natural) sciences, if the latter are construed in realist terms.

[50] These experiments involve disrupting the expectations of participants in everyday situations. In one, students repeatedly required their victims to clarify the meaning of their remarks. Others behaved in their own homes as if they were polite boarders. On another occasion, they were instructed to act on the assumption that their interlocutor was trying to deceive them. In most cases the response of the victims was acute annoyance as well as a certain bewilderment. See H. Garfinkel, *Studies in Ethnomethodology* (Hemel Hempstead, Prentice-Hall, 1967), pp. 35–75.

[51] H. P. Dreitzel (ed.), *Recent Sociology No. 2. Patterns of Communicative Behaviour* (New York, Macmillan, 1970), p. xvf.

language. I cannot discuss the former alternative here; the latter, however, develops in an interesting way some earlier tendencies of 'classical' *verstehende* sociology.

Much to the surprise of its somewhat blinkered practitioners, the philosophical technique known as 'linguistic analysis' has suggested some extremely radical ways of looking at human behaviour. One can perhaps distinguish two main currents: the first, relatively 'moderate', is concerned to show, on the basis of a careful study of the way we explain actions, that, for instance, 'motives' are to be distinguished from 'causes' in that they are conceptually or logically related to the actions of which they are the motives.[52] This underlying tendency has thrown up a second, more radical offshoot in the form of Peter Winch's book.[53] Winch's 'idea of a social science' can perhaps best be understood as behaviourism stood on its head. Whereas behaviourists reduce speech to behaviour, Winch reduces behaviour to speech by treating it as a form of communication governed by rules; social relations are 'like' logical relations between propositions.[54]

We have already seen a hint of this approach in Wittgenstein's insight that what distinguishes human behaviour from that of animals is that humans can in principle talk about what they do. In a sense they can only 'do' what they can in principle talk about. Human actions are intersubjectively identifiable (Weber's 'direct understanding') because in order to be actions at all they must be able to be conceptualised in a public language. The transcendental investigation of the 'basic rules of everyday life' which seemed so problematic for phenomenology, can be carried out in the form of an empirical investigation of language. 'Linguistic investigations were always empirically directed logical analyses. *Verstehende* sociology is now also consigned to this level.'[55]

I cannot go further into the philosophical details of the alleged relationship between 'language-game' and 'form of life', logical and social relations, on which this approach is based. Its implications for *verstehende* sociology are, however, interestingly brought out in

---

[52] This is just one of the ways in which contemporary analytic philosophy has reacted against the positivist tradition out of which it originally grew. See Karl-Otto Apel, *Analytic Philosophy of Language and the Geisteswissenschaften* (Dordrecht, Reidel, 1967), *passim*. Cf. also G. H. von Wright, *Explanation and Understanding* (London, Routledge, 1972), Chapter 1.

[53] P. Winch, *The Idea of a Social Science and its Relation to Philosophy* (London, Routledge, 1958).

[54] ibid., p. 126.   [55] Habermas, op. cit., p. 221.

Winch's criticisms of Weber.[56] First, however, it is worth noticing that they would both agree in condemning Durkheim's *démarche* at the beginning of '*Suicide*'. As Winch puts it:

'It is particularly important to notice the connection between Durkheim's conclusion—that conscious deliberations may be treated as "purely formal, with no object but confirmation of a resolve previously formed for reasons unknown to consciousness"—and his initial decision to define the word "suicide" in a sense different from that which it bore within the societies which he was studying.'[57]

Alasdair MacIntyre has worked out in more detail how Durkheim's definition of suicide 'entails the irrelevance of the agent's reasons in the explanation of suicide'.[58] But he also makes the point that it does not follow 'that all such decisions to bring actions under descriptions other than those used by the agents themselves are bound to lead to the same *a priori* obliteration of the explanatory role of reasons; for this obliteration was in Durkheim's case . . . a consequence of certain special features of his treatment of the concept of suicide, and not a consequence of any general feature of the procedure of inventing new descriptive terms in social science.'[59]

Winch's first criticism of Weber is that he 'often speaks as if the ultimate test [of whether or not we have understood a piece of behaviour] . . . were our ability to formulate statistical laws which would enable us to *predict* with fair accuracy what people would be likely to do in given circumstances'.[60] But, Winch argues, Wittgenstein's deviant timber merchants[61] show that this does not guarantee understanding. 'Understanding in situations like this, is grasping the *point* or the *meaning* of what is being done or said. This is a notion far removed from the world of statistics and causal laws: it is closer

[56] Winch, op. cit., pp. 111–20.

[57] ibid., p. 111; cf. E. Durkheim, *Suicide* (London, Routledge, 1952).

[58] A. MacIntyre, 'The Idea of a Social Science', *Proceedings of the Aristotelian Society* (supplementary volume, 1967), p. 107. Reprinted in A. MacIntyre, *Against the Self-Images of the Age* (London, Duckworth, 1971) and in A. Ryan (ed.), *The Philosophy of Social Explanation* (Oxford University Press, 1973).

[59] ibid., p. 108.

[60] Winch, op. cit., p. 115.

[61] Ludwig Wittgenstein, *Remarks on the Foundations of Mathematics* (Oxford, Blackwell, 1956), pp. 142–51. The timber merchants in Wittgenstein's imaginary society 'piled the timber in heaps of arbitrary varying height and then sold it at a price proportionate to the area covered by the piles. And what if they even justified this with the words: "Of course, if you buy more timber, you must pay more"?'

to the realm of discourse and to the internal relations that link the parts of a realm of discourse.'[62]

But one must bear in mind that Weber was thinking of a situation in which the social scientist is confronted by a plurality of explanations, all of them equally *verständlich* or even 'evident'. And whatever the difficulties of applying Weber's solution in practice, it does seem to be the only answer to questions about motivation. Winch believes that identifying the correct answer to such questions can *only* be a conceptual problem, that 'Sociologists who misinterpret an alien culture are like philosophers getting into difficulties over the use of their own concepts.'[63] But what is one to say about cases in which alternative explanations are all equally under-written by the *Lebensform*? What can one do other than manipulate by thought-experiment the various factors in the context of motivation in order to yield testable predictions? It does seem to be the case that 'to ask whether it was the agent's reason that roused him to act is to ask a causal question'.[64] The antithesis between motives and causes 'may not in fact be so stark as recent philosophical discussion has tended to make it'.[65]

Winch's second objection is the related one that Weber denies that there is any

'logical difference between the technique of manipulating natural objects (e.g. machinery) in order to achieve one's ends and that of "manipulating" human beings as, he suggests, does the owner of a factory his employees. He says "that in the one case 'events of consciousness' enter into the causal chain and in the other case not, makes 'logically' not the slightest difference"; thus committing the mistake of supposing that "events of consciousness" just happen to differ empirically from other kinds of event. He does not realise that the whole notion of an "event" carries a different sense here, implying as it does a context of humanly followed rules which cannot be combined with a context of causal laws in this way without creating logical difficulties.'[66]

Winch points out that

'In trying to describe the situation he is using as an example in such a way as to support his point of view, Weber ceases to use the notions that

[62] Winch, op. cit., p. 115.   [63] ibid., p. 114.
[64] MacIntyre, op. cit., p. 100.
[65] W. G. Runciman, *A Critique of Max Weber's Philosophy of Social Science* (Cambridge University Press, 1972), p. 26.
[66] Winch, op. cit., pp. 116f.

would be appropriate to an interpretative understanding of the situation. Instead of speaking of the workers in his factory being paid and spending money, he speaks of their being handed pieces of metal, handing these pieces of metal over to other people and receiving objects from them. . . . In short, he adopts the external point of view and forgets to take account of the "subjectively intended sense" of the behaviour he is talking about.'[67]

But as MacIntyre has shown, there is no need for Weber implicitly to concede Winch's point in this way. It might be possible, for example, to reduce trade union activity in a factory either: (*a*) by selectively offering opportunities for overtime; or (*b*) by moving workers from one part of the factory to another. In the former case, the workers' reasons 'can find a place in the explanation without its losing its causal character', while it remains the case that 'true causal explanations cannot be formulated—where actions are concerned—unless intentions, motives and reasons are taken into account'.[68]

These are just two points at which Winch's thesis seems doubtful. But having referred to these detailed criticisms, it is worth considering what would follow if Winch were right. Despite some of his more paradoxical assertions, it is hardly fair to say that he wants to make sociology an *a priori* science; if he suggests that it should conform more closely to the practice of anthropology, getting to know a community in depth and interpreting it (at least initially) in its own terms, this is not necessarily a bad thing. To Winch's credit, he no more seeks to evade the charge of relativism than that of idealism.

I do not wish to discuss the philosophical paradoxes of relativism, nor the practical limitations it would impose on social science.[69] I am interested rather in the possibility that even to attempt a seriously relativistic approach is beyond the powers of a social scientist who operates within a given historical context.

[67] ibid., p. 117.
[68] MacIntyre, op. cit., p. 109.
[69] There is an excellent discussion of some of these problems in an article by Ernest Gellner, 'Concepts and Society', *Transactions of the Fifth World Congress of Sociology*, Vol. 1 (Louvain, 1962), reprinted in D. Emmet and A. MacIntyre (eds), *Sociological Theory and Philosophical Analysis* (London, Macmillan, 1970). Gellner writes: 'It is *not* true to say that to understand the concepts of a society (in the way its members do) is to understand the society. Concepts are as liable to mask reality as to reveal it, and masking some of it may be a part of their function' (in Emmet and MacIntyre, op. cit., p. 148, n. 1).

Winch, like his master Wittgenstein, is confronted by a dilemma. Either every form of life is shut off from every other,[70] which seems implausible, or one must postulate 'a metalanguage to mediate the analysed language-games'.[71]

> 'Winch seems to have in mind a linguistic version of Dilthey. From his free-floating position the language-analyst can slip at will into the grammar of all language games, without himself being tied to the dogma of his own language-game which would impose conditions on linguistic analysis as such.'[72]

But this is the same 'objectivistic' illusion that we find in positivist science.[73] Unless he can find a meta-language into which the grammar of all natural languages could be translated Winch commits himself to an essentially hermeneutic process of the mutual interpretation of language-games from which the historical situation of the analyst cannot be methodologically excluded—it can at best be negotiated in what Gadamer calls the 'melting of horizons'.[74]

My assessment of the social theories discussed in the last few sections has drawn heavily on Jürgen Habermas's analysis in *Zur Logik der Sozialwissenschaften*. Habermas's position, which is ably presented by Albrecht Wellmer[75] can perhaps be summarised in the following points:

1. The data of social science are already partially interpreted in everyday life and ordinary language. The 'intentional' character of social action and social relations can only be grasped through an interpretative or '*verstehende*' procedure, 'through the medium of communication'.[76]
2. Attempts to make the interpretative procedure described in point 1 merely the prolegomena to a 'general theory of society', an interrelated body of lawlike generalisations, seem to come up against problems of principle.

---

[70] Cf. MacIntyre, op. cit.
[71] Albrecht Wellmer, *Critical Theory of Society* (New York, Herder & Herder, 1971), p. 30.
[72] Habermas, op. cit., pp. 243f.
[73] Cf. Habermas, *Knowledge and Human Interests* (London, Heinemann, 1972), pp. 178ff.
[74] Habermas, *Zur Logik der Sozialwissenschaften*, p. 245.
[75] A. Wellmer, op. cit.
[76] ibid., p. 35; cf. the paper by Talcott Parsons in O. Stammer (ed.), *Max Weber and Sociology Today* (Oxford, Blackwell, 1971).

'One difficulty is that to date no one has discovered any really universal social laws, and that, where they have been thought to have been uncovered, they have lost all specifically social content and consequently all specifically social explanatory value. To a certain extent, the situation in the social sciences would appear to be the converse of that obtaining in the physical sciences: the more universal the laws, the more devoid of content they become, or rather, the less explanatory value they have. The second difficulty is the result of the attempt to measure social facts: there is no satisfactory and universally valid operationalisation of theoretical principles in the social sciences.'[77]

Taken together, points 1 and 2 suggests a certain rapprochement between 'social science' and 'common sense'.

3. Wittgenstein's shift of allegiance from the universal scientific language of his *Tractatus*[78] to the 'ordinary language' of the *Investigations*[79] led to a revival of interest in the idea of '*sprachverstehende*' sociology. Wittgenstein's plurality of 'forms of life' is a modern equivalent of the concepts of 'linguistic community' (*Sprachgemeinschaft*) and 'objective mind' which underwrites earlier attempts at the non-causal interpretation of social and cultural phenomena. But this approach leads to a relativism, a 'monadology of language-games', not essentially different from the subjectivism of phenomenological analyses.

4. An interpretative method, whether based on phenomenological premises or on those of linguistic philosophy, cannot take account of the coercive causal influences on human life. MacIntyre has criticised Winch in the following terms:

'If Winch were correct, and rule-governed behaviour was not to be understood as causal behaviour, then the contrast could not be drawn between those cases in which the relation of social structure to individuals may be correctly characterised in terms of control and constraint and those in which it may not.'[80]

Habermas puts it more generally:

'A *verstehende* sociology which hypostatises language so as to make it the subject of the form of life and the tradition ties itself to the idealist premise that linguistically articulated consciousness determines the material meaning of life-activity. But the objective system (*Zusammen-*

[77] loc. cit.
[78] L. Wittgenstein, *Tractatus Logico-Philosophicus* (London, Kegan Paul, 1923).
[79] Wittgenstein, *Philosophical Investigations*.
[80] MacIntyre, op. cit., p. 103.

hang) of social action is not confined to the dimension of inter-subjectively intended and symbolically transmitted meaning. The linguistic infrastructure of society is a moment of a system which, however they are mediated symbolically, is also constituted by the constraints of reality; the constraint of external nature which goes into the process of technical control (*Verfügung*) and the constraint of inner nature reflected in the repressions of social power relations. . . . Sociology cannot allow itself to be reduced to being merely interpretative.'[81]

The above points are all underpinned, in different ways, by arguments derived from Hans-Georg Gadamer's hermeneutics. Much of Gadamer's *Wahrheit und Methode* (*Truth and Method*)[82] consists of a substantial critique of the *Geisteswissenschaft* tradition which, in contrast to earlier hermeneutic theories, systematically neglected the question of the truth of the material it interpreted.[83] Gadamer's loyalties are to Hegel (mediated by Heidegger) rather than Schleiermacher.[84] His concept of *Verstehen*, secondly, embodies the important concept of *Wirkungsgeschichte*, the 'real' historical processes through which the historical material of the 'tradition' is handed down and applied.

> 'The thesis of my book is that the real-historical moment is effective and remains effective in all understanding of tradition, even where the "method" of the modern historical sciences has established itself and made what-has-become [*das Gewordene*], the historical tradition, into an object to be "identified" [*festzustellen*] like an experimental finding as though the tradition were as alien and, from a human point of view, incomprehensible as the objects of physics.'[85]

(It is this approach which he and Habermas call 'objectivistic'.)

His aim, Gadamer says,[86] is not to recommend 'unscientific "*engagement*"' but rather the "scientific" seriousness which admits the *engagement* which is effective in all understanding.'

The relation between this existentialist hermeneutics and the 'critical theory' of Habermas and others, is extremely difficult to specify.[87] Habermas welcomes Gadamer's criticisms of the 'objectivistic self-understanding of the *Geisteswissenschaften*' (which

---

[81] Habermas, *Zur Logik der Sozialwissenschaften*, p. 289.

[82] Hans-Georg Gadamer, *Wahrheit und Methode* (Tübingen, Mohr, 1960, 2nd edition 1965).

[83] Gadamer, op. cit. (2nd edn), pp. 162ff. Cf. Wellmer, op. cit., pp. 42ff.

[84] ibid., p. 162.   [85] ibid., p. xix.

[86] ibid., p. x.

[87] The best available account is in Wellmer, op. cit., pp. 31–51.

he says also apply to the movement's 'phenomenological and linguistic executors')[88] and also his stress on the historical involvement of the 'observer' and the internal connection between hermeneutic understanding and application.[89] In Wellmer's words:

'One of the most important contributions of hermeneutical thought is the destruction of the objectivistic pretension of the historico-hermeneutical sciences, among which a language-interpretative sociology might be counted. By seeing the scientist and the object of his research as linked by a context of tradition, hermeneutical thought discovers in the process of mediation (that is, the interpretative explication of historically evolving forms of life), the practical life-interests which, as such, cannot be discarded and are operative in the scientist's initial insight.'[90]

Part of this 'objectivistic illusion', it may be suggested, is the belief that the meaning of actions is no more than their subjectively intended meaning, which can be elicited by psychological insight. Hermeneutical interpretation of course requires the concept of 'objective meaning'. 'In contrast to purely language-analytical interpretative sociology, hermeneutical theory justifies attempts at a functionalist, ideology-critical or psychoanalytical description of objectively meaningful social relations.'[91]

This, in general terms, is the problem with which Habermas ended *Zur Logik der Sozialwissenschaften*, and which has continued to preoccupy him in more recent years. The unifying theme of his investigations may be said to be the idea that the notion of *Verstehen*, conceived in universalistic terms, presupposes not only that linguistic communication be free from psychopathological or ideological distortion, but also that the whole society be organised in a way which approximates to an 'unconstrained dialogue', in other words, that what goes on in that society is a matter of rational reflection and discussion, and not the product of mysterious causal mechanisms whose operation is believed to be inevitable. It is in this sense that Gadamer's hermeneutics is claimed to 'require the hypothetical anticipation of a philosophy of history with practical intent'.[92]

Speculative arguments of this sort are complemented by a more concrete analysis of 'communicative competence' which represents

[88] Habermas, *Zur Logik der Sozialwissenschaften*, p. 265.
[89] ibid., p. 275.   [90] Wellmer, op. cit., pp. 32f.
[91] ibid., p. 33.
[92] Habermas, *Zur Logik der Sozialwissenschaften*, p. 290.

Ideologiekritik (the Marxist-inspired criticism of ideology) as being, like psychoanalysis, both a theory of and a therapy for 'systematically distorted communication'. Psychoanalytic theory, Habermas claims, involves a mixture of interpretation and causal explanation.[93] It starts from a breakdown of intersubjective communication common enough in everyday interaction, when one gives up trying to understand what one's interlocutor is 'getting at', and looks rather for a causal explanation of his unintelligible discourse or conduct. By uncovering unconscious motives which have causal force just because they are unconscious,[94] the psychoanalytic dialogue allows the patient to overcome them. Intersubjectivity is restored in both discourse and action.

I have not been able here to do justice to the complexities of Habermas's thought, but the theoretical framework within which he cast his discussion of modern social theory is, in my view, by far the most interesting available. It is encouraging that his work is now receiving closer attention outside the German-speaking world.

[93] Habermas, *Knowledge and Human Interests*, Chs 10–12.
[94] Habermas, *Zur Logik der Sozialwissenschaften*, p. 297.

7

Conclusion

What, in conclusion, can be said about the relationship between these recent developments in social thought and the historical controversy over *Verstehen*? The concept, as we have seen, had its origins in theological hermeneutics, in attempts to clarify the meaning of historical texts, and it has been claimed that social phenomena are in an important sense analogous to texts.[1] Two points can be made about this activity of clarification. Firstly, it is generally not a matter of attaining *the* correct reading of a particular passage, though this may be the case where one is simply concerned with linguistic meaning. More frequently, there is a choice between a number of more or less plausible interpretations. As Simmel suggested,[2] these different interpretations of a historical or literary phenomenon may not rule one another out even in principle; alternatively, we may say that even if they are in principle contradictory, there is no procedure for deciding between the various alternatives such as exist in sciences which operate by some process of verification. The second point is that in some cases one might want to argue that it is anyway mistaken to see this as a matter of 'restoring' the pristine meaning of a text; what is involved is, rather, a *creative* process of interpretation by which a researcher makes available to his contemporaries material from an earlier society or one which is culturally 'alien'.

This is the view of hermeneutics which is common to Gadamer and Habermas. The latter, as we have seen,[3] criticised Dilthey for

---

[1] Cf. Charles Taylor, 'Interpretation and the Sciences of Man', *Review of Metaphysics* (1971).

[2] see above, p. 45.

[3] see above, pp. 34f.

his tendency to obliterate these features of the hermeneutic enterprise by flirting with a psychological account of it.

'Hermeneutic understanding ties the interpreter to the role of partner in dialogue. Only this model of *participation in communication learned in interaction* can explain the specific achievement of hermeneutics. Yet Dilthey never abandoned the contrary model of empathy, of basically solitary reproduction and re-experiencing, even in its modified form of the reconstruction of acts of meaning-creation. . . . Dilthey cannot free himself from the empathy model of understanding because, despite his Kantian orientation, he does not succeed in overcoming the contemplative concept of truth. *Re-experiencing* is in a significant sense the equivalent of observation. . . .'[4]

The contrary view, which Habermas derived from Gadamer, is that the researcher cannot isolate himself from his own 'horizon'. Objectivity can be achieved only through the 'melting of horizons' in communication.[5]

Dilthey never achieved his projected 'foundation of the human sciences'. One can speculate about what the finished system might have looked like, but it seems unlikely that the contradictory pressures of positivistic psychologism and German idealism would have allowed him to achieve a lasting synthesis. Much has changed in intellectual life since Dilthey's time. The social sciences, which were then in their infancy (with the possible exception of economics) are now, whatever else they may be, an ongoing enterprise. Secondly, there is a much greater awareness of the place of language in making understanding possible. Much of what Dilthey wrote about the 'objective mind' might today be cast in linguistic terms. Thirdly, until recently at least, there seemed a less favourable climate for speculative thought. But the attempt to separate the social from the natural sciences, what Habermas has called 'the suppressed complex of scientific dualism',[6] is still very much alive. If anything, it has returned in a yet more radical form. *Verstehen* was conceived by Simmel and Weber in largely psychological terms; both writers, in different ways, gloss over the problems of the understanding of meaning. What has happened in the last decade or two is a reversion to a more full-blooded emphasis on the hermeneutic basis of any

[4] J. Habermas, *Knowledge and Human Interests* (London, Heinemann, 1972), pp. 179ff.

[5] This can be seen in Habermas's criticisms of Winch (above, pp. 98ff).

[6] J. Habermas, *Zur Logik der Sozialwissenschaften* (Frankfurt, Suhrkamp, 1970) p. 72.

account of social life. Some important movements in social thought seem to be going back beyond Weber to Dilthey, or at least to certain general preoccupations which Dilthey shared with other nineteenth- and early twentieth-century writers. The 'phenomenological' movement in sociology still cultivates a rather confused relationship with Husserl, whose influence on Dilthey's later work was considerable. They both had an important influence on the later Wittgenstein. As I suggested above (pp. 43, 99) there is a strong analogy between Dilthey's *objective mind*, Husserl's *Lebenswelt* and Wittgenstein's linguistic community tied to a *form of life*. All three are aimed at warding off the collapse into a solipsistic individualism and explaining the possibility of satisfactory communication in a public language. But the only real advance seems to lie in the greater awareness of the importance of language in Wittgenstein and other later writers. The central question, whether a full-blooded *verstehende* approach can be combined with causal explanation, or whether it can, on its own, sustain a social science, remains open.[7]

As I suggested above,[8] Weber's compromise between the rival claims of understanding and causal explanation has proved unstable in important respects. Weber appears to hesitate between two versions. In one, *Verstehen* yields a hypothesis which can be verified by causal investigation. But his account of causation, centred around the notion of causal imputation (*Zurechnung*), seems too open-ended to perform this task. In the second version, which seems both more coherent and more easily identified in his substantive work, *Verstehen* allows one to assimilate an action to an ideal-typical 'context of motivation' such as that of rational economic action. As Weber implies in the essay on Roscher and Knies,[9] these motivational schemata cannot be seen as *hypotheses* in any very literal sense, since 'the statement that they do not in any concrete case contain a valid interpretation does not impugn their interpretative value'.[10] But if this is the case, the assimilation of an action to any such scheme remains problematic, depending only on the observer's judgement.

The problems this raises were ably discussed by Schutz, and these

[7] Cf. K.-O. Apel, *Analytic Philosophy of Language and the Geisteswissenschaften* (Dordrecht, Reidel, 1967); and G. H. von Wright, *Explanation and Understanding* (London, Routledge, 1971).
[8] see above, pp. 52ff.
[9] M. Weber, *Gesammelte Aufsätze zur Wissenschaftslehre* (Tübingen, Mohr, 1922), pp. 1–145. A useful extract from this essay is reprinted in A. Giddens (ed.), *Positivism and Sociology* (London, Heinemann, 1974), pp. 23–31.
[10] ibid., p. 26.

issues have been taken up by 'phenomenological sociologists' such as Peter Berger and by 'ethnomethodologists'. The latter movement is extremely difficult to identify; Harold Garfinkel, who coined the term 'ethnomethodology', laments the fact that it has become a shibboleth,[11] and the editor of a recent 'reader' in the field admits that 'It is possible that some of the researchers here represented would not (or would no longer) characterise their work as ethnomethodology.'[12] In general, though, I think it is fair to see it as a species of phenomenological sociology, sharing a complex agglomerate of more or less explicit theoretical and methodological principles (to which I have referred above) and employing a style which ranges uneasily between the extremes of 'hip' informality and pretentious neologism. In this very broad 'phenomenological' current, one can see the purest modern form of a *verstehende* sociology. It is characterised by an emphasis on the 'subjective meanings' of social agents and the way in which 'social structure' is built up out of a plurality of 'definitions of the situation'; the question of the objective reality of that social structure is left in abeyance. As we have seen, Habermas criticised the phenomenological tradition, from Schutz to Garfinkel and Cicourel, for its subjectivism (traceable back to its concept of meaning)[13] and its neglect of language. More recently, however, Cicourel has been directly concerned with socio-linguistic problems.[14] Whereas he was previously concerned with the 'negotiation of reality' by means of 'accounting procedures' which only *happened* to be linguistic in form, the problem is now how we acquire (a sense of) social structure as part of the process of learning a language.

There remains though, the crucial equivocation between talking

[11] H. Garfinkel, 'The Origins of the Term "Ethnomethodology",' reprinted in Roy Turner (ed.), *Ethnomethodology* (Harmondsworth, Penguin Books, 1974), p. 18.

[12] ibid., p. 7.

[13] I do not think that this means that a phenomenological analysis of social processes is merely psychological. At the extreme, it might be held that the aim was simply to give a descriptive account of people's views of a situation, without saying anything about either logical contradictions between different views or about the influence that one view may exert on another. But writers in this tradition seem more often to be concerned precisely with the interplay of different definitions and, as I suggested above, with the way in which what we call 'social reality' is determined by that interplay and the consensus that may result from it.

[14] Cf. his paper entitled 'The Acquisition of Social Structure: Towards a Developmental Sociology of Language and Meaning' in A. Cicourel, *Cognitive Sociology* (Harmondsworth, Penguin Books, 1973).

about people's 'sense of social structure' and talking about social structure itself. And while social structure is of course partly a consequence of the way people *perceive* social relations it is clearly more than this. One can, of course, conceive social situations in very different ways, but as Dreitzel[15] puts it, in the language of critical theory: 'the limitations of the human capacity to create intersubjective worlds can only be studied when the reductionism of ethnomethodology is avoided; the social world is not only structured by language but also by the modes and forces of material production and by the system of domination'. Phenomenological sociologists sometimes claim to be more radical, in both an epistemological and a political sense, than adherents of 'positivist' sociology who 'take the objective character of the social world for granted'.[16] 'By virtue of its reliance on the common-sense view of the social world as real, positivistic sociology is effectively engaged in an elaboration of this common-sense view and may be correctly described as a species of folk wisdom.'[17] But the radicalism of phenomenology seems to be spurious. Of course a radical theory of society must call into question social arrangements and beliefs which have been previously considered inescapable, but they cannot be changed merely by pointing out the mechanism by which they are maintained. To say that the emperor is naked is to make an empirical claim, which can at best be complemented by an analysis of why his nakedness had not previously been noticed. An extreme ethnomethodologist would say that it is up to us whether we choose to see a clothed or an unclothed emperor; he would thus give some support to those subversives who took the latter view, but he would not help them in any way to substantiate their claim against those who took the former view.

A phenomenological approach seems most helpful where the concepts in terms of which a situation is defined are not neutral between the participants but pertain to and serve the interests of one side. It has thus generated some interesting studies in the so-called 'sociology of deviance', which tends to study situations in which inarticulate 'criminals', 'madmen' or whatever are confronted by highly integrated legal and medical systems and their associated ideologies. In such a context, merely to suggest the possibility of an

[15] H. P. Dreitzel (ed.), *Recent Sociology No. 2. Patterns of Communicative Behaviour* (New York, Macmillan, 1970), p. xvii.
[16] David Walsh, 'Sociology and the Social World', in P. Filmer *et al.*, *New Directions in Sociological Theory* (London, Collier-Macmillan, 1972), p. 27.
[17] ibid., p. 28.

alternative 'definition of the situation' (such as one which the 'deviants' themselves would give) may be a subversive, radical act. But a genuinely critical social theory must be able to make objective claims about reality, and it is no accident that Marxists have generally been as sharp to attack traces of relativism as the most hard-boiled positivist.

Modern analytic philosophy, in the course of its 'immanent critique' of logical positivism, has provided another source of support for a *verstehende* position. Very roughly, attempts to construct formalised 'scientific' languages were abandoned in favour of a closer analysis of the structure and oversuppositions of 'ordinary language'. Charles Taylor, R. S. Peters, Alasdair MacIntyre and others have given a new legitimacy to explanations of action in 'everyday' terms, in other words in terms of intentions, motives, purposes etc. Peter Winch, drawing more directly on the later Wittgenstein (and coming closer to phenomenological discussions of the *Lebenswelt*) gives a more radical, and perhaps ultimately incoherent twist to these claims. Winch's *Idea of a Social Science* has interested philosophers, and social scientists in their more reflective moments, but it has had little practical effect on social research, except perhaps to encourage certain trends in social anthropology which were already well established—in particular, the 'indiscriminately charitable' attitude to alien beliefs which Ernest Gellner criticised in his important article, 'Concepts and Society'.[18] This attitude, Gellner suggests, has intellectual roots in functionalism and an ideological foundation in 'the tolerant, understanding liberalism, of which sophisticated anthropology is a part'.[19]

It is hard to say if this is a necessary consequence of a *verstehende* position; though such a position might be taken to mean that a society can only be understood in its own terms, one could reasonably suggest that members of that society might find alien concepts (the concept of ideology, for instance) useful in analysing their situation. Winch seems to place unwarranted restrictions on conceptual changes of this sort. Stan Cohen and Laurie Taylor's *Psychological Survival*[20] exemplifies this strategy, which goes some

[18] Transactions of the Fifth World Congress of Sociologists. Reprinted in D. Emmet and A. MacIntyre (eds), *Sociological Theory and Philosophical Analysis* (London, Macmillan, 1970).

[19] ibid., p. 128.

[20] S. Cohen and L. Taylor, *Psychological Survival. The Experience of Long-Term Imprisonment* (Harmondsworth, Penguin Books, 1972).

way to answering the charge that a *verstehende* sociology 'leaves the world as it is'.

There is a more general point to be made about the relevance of social anthropology. It is no accident that Winch's book was seen as more relevant to the concerns of 'anthropologists' than to those of 'sociologists'. The problems involved in the 'direct understanding' of social phenomena are more obvious where the researcher is working in an 'alien' society whose language and customs differ radically from those of his own society. The partial (and long overdue) *rapprochement* of sociology and anthropology in recent years has encouraged a more sophisticated awareness of these problems, which are clearly relevant even to sociologists working within their own cultural area.[21]

Modern social thought is in a pluralistic, even anarchic state. Some of the changes which have taken place in recent years could perhaps be explained in terms of the internal development of theories; it might be argued that movements like logical positivism, behaviourism and structural-functional system theory declined because they had outlived their usefulness as 'paradigms', though the last two, at least, could hardly be said to have any clearly defined and generally accepted successors.

Only 'structuralism' and Marxism remain at all fashionable as ways of integrating the social sciences into some general theory of society. I cannot discuss the protean theoretical current of structuralism at this point, though it may be worth saying that despite the arguments of its adherents, conducted at an extremely high level of generality, the distinctiveness of the method remains in some doubt.[22] As regards the questions discussed here, part of the appeal of structuralism may lie in the claim that it enables one to avoid certain types of causal question, or at least reformulate them in a more sophisticated way. To speak of relations of correspondence or homology between structures, and even of logical transformations, is to avoid questions about the causal mechanisms involved. One such mechanism, it might be argued, is human activity or *praxis*.

[21] Cf. also A. Cicourel, *Method and Measurement in Sociology* (Glencoe, Free Press, 1964).

[22] Cf. W. G. Runciman, 'What is Structuralism?', *British Journal of Sociology* (1969). Reprinted in A. Ryan (ed.), *The Philosophy of Social Explanation* (Oxford University Press, 1973). Useful general books on structuralism are J. Piaget, *Structuralism* (London, Routledge, 1971); and M. Lane (ed.), *Structuralism: A Reader* (London, Cape, 1970).

Goldmann's structuralism, as we have seen, claimed to take account of these considerations, but this concern is less evident in the work of other structuralists. So far, at least, the structuralism seems confined to giving more or less plausible accounts of certain 'super-structural' relationships.

The nature of contemporary Marxism and its place in modern social thought is equally hard to define. All one can say is that there has been a considerable revival of interest in Marxism, both in the work of Lukács and of the Frankfurt school (which has only recently become readily accessible to Anglo-Saxon readers) and in the 'scientific' Marxism of the Althusserians. (It need hardly be emphasised that Britain and the United States remain heavily dependent on 'continental' theorists.) If one represents academic sociology and political science in the post-war years as a 'cold war' between functionalism and Marxism, it must be seen as a war in which the latter was barely present in any serious form and was at best felt as an influence in the work of Wright Mills or of the so-called 'conflict theorists'. Clearly the situation has changed, though it is too early to say what will develop; most recent work has consisted of methodological criticism or of primarily theoretical studies such as Nicos Poulantzas's *Political Power and Social Classes*.[23] Some social scientists await a new theoretical 'paradigm' which will permit the integration and perhaps even axiomatisation of all systematic knowledge about human society. Others consider that the paradigm, Marxist, structuralist or phenomenological, already exists in embryo and needs only to be elaborated, while more sceptical researchers are content to fossick around in a research tradition defined by the available quantitative techniques or to deposit their offerings in or around the temples of Marx, Weber or Durkheim. At present the clearest trend, though it is by no means universal, is towards scepticism about the ways in which 'scientific' theories of society have been conceived, and a closer attention to problems of description and interpretation. But it would be a mistake to see the revival of interest in a *verstehende* approach to social life purely in terms of theoretical developments. Growing scepticism about the claims of functionalism has at least been fed by a more general doubt about the directions in which the 'advanced' societies are in fact advancing. Charles Taylor has suggested that 'The

[23] N. Poulantzas, *Political Power and Social Classes* (London, New Left Books, 1973).

strains in contemporary society, the breakdown of civility, the rise of deep alienation, which is translated into even more destructive action, tend to shake the basic categories of our social science. . . .[24] My principal claim is that we can only come to grips with this phenomenon of breakdown by trying to understand more clearly and profoundly the common and intersubjective meanings of the society in which we have been living.'[25]

I have tried to show that a decision about the proper place of an interpretative method in social theory involves fundamental choices about the proper purposes of such theories. Do we want a coherent system of general social laws, or a plurality of 'theories of the middle range', or just a few isolated by well-confirmed conditional propositions? Or are we more concerned to deepen and systematise and enrich with empirical data the understanding of social life that we already have as participants? Do we want knowledge for the sake of prediction and control, or for the intrinsic pleasure of cultured contemplation, or to orientate the political action of a social group or movement?

Few people would deny, though some would consider it uninteresting, that the *starting-point* of social inquiry is some sort of intersubjective understanding. This is not merely to affirm that ordinary language is the ultimate meta-language of any science (a claim that might be questioned in the case of some of the more highly mathematised natural sciences); it is rather that we begin in the *Lebenswelt*, talking 'everyday language' and using 'everyday accounting procedures'. This initial situation, I would argue, has a different significance for the social than for the natural sciences; the former take their concepts from everyday life from the language which is common to them and their objects of investigation, and their explanatory principles remain extremely close to those of everyday life. Where social scientists have strayed too far from 'commonsense' constructs, the result has been not greater sophistication, but trivialisation.

This does not mean that a social science which was in any sense empirical could be sustained by *verstehende* methods alone. Again, few people would disagree in principle, but when one discusses what would count as a satisfactory research programme the differences

[24] Taylor, op. cit., p. 40ff.
[25] ibid., p. 44. At another level, Dreitzel has suggested certain parallels between the disruptive experiments of Garfinkel and others and the confrontation tactics of student militants (Dreitzel, op. cit., pp. xviiff.).

return. At times what is visible on the surface is merely the choice between different *styles* of theorising, but behind the choice of style lie more fundamental questions about the purpose of social theory, to which there is perhaps no single right answer.

Bibliography

1a) Central Texts of the *Verstehen* Tradition in History and Social Thought

WILHELM DILTHEY
Historik (Munich/Berlin, Oldenbourg, 1937); incorporates the *Grundriss*. *Gesammelte Schriften (GS)* Leipzig and Berlin, Teubner. See in particular: '*Einleitung in die Geisteswissenschaften*' (Vol. 1); '*Die Entstehung der Hermeneutik*' (Vol. 5); '*Der Aufbau der Geschichtlichen Welt in den Geisteswissenschaften*' (Vol. 7).
Das Erlebnis und die Dichtung (Leipzig, Teubner, 1910).

J. G. DROYSEN
Grundriss der Historik (Halle-Saale, Niemeyer, 1925). First published in 1858. This has been translated as *Outlines of the Principles of History* (Boston, Ginn & Co., 1893).

HEINRICH RICKERT
Die Grenzen der naturwissenschaftlichen Begriffsbildung (Tübingen, Mohr, 3rd/4th edn 1921), first pub. 1902.
Science and History (New York, Van Nostrand, 1962), first pub. 1899 as *Kulturwissenschaft und Naturwissenschaft*.

ALFRED SCHUTZ
The Phenomenology of the Social World (London, Heinemann, 1972), first pub. 1932 as *Der sinnhafte Aufbau der sozialen Welt. Eine Einführung in die verstehende Soziologie.*

GEORG SIMMEL
Probleme der Geschichtsphilosophie (Leipzig, Duncker & Humblot, 5th edn. first pub. 1892).
'*Vom Wesen des historischen Verstehens*', *Brücke und Tür* (Stuttgart, Koehler, 1957).
Essays on Sociology, Philosophy and Aesthetics, Kurt Wolff (ed.) (New York, Harper & Row, 1965).
The Sociology of Georg Simmel, Kurt Wolff (ed.) (Glencoe, Free Press, 1950).

MAX WEBER
Economy and Society (New York, Bedminster, 1968), first pub. posthumously 1922 as *Grundriss der Sozialökonomik: Wirtschaft und Gesellschaft.*
Gesammelte Aufsätze zur Wissenschaftslehre (GAW) (Tübingen, Mohr, 1922).
The Methodology of the Social Sciences, eds. E. Shils and H. A. Finch (Glencoe, Free Press, 1949).
Religionssoziologie (RS) (Tübingen, Mohr, 1920, 2 vols).
Gesammelte Aufsätze zur Soziologie und Sozialpolitik (GASS) (Tübingen, Mohr, 1924).
The Protestant Ethic and the Spirit of Capitalism (Lon-

H

don, Allen & Unwin, 1971), Trans. Talcott Parsons of essays originally published in 1904 and 1905.

WILHELM WINDELBAND   *Geschichte und Naturwissenschaft* (Strasbourg, 1894).

1b) Introductions to These Works, and General Historical Surveys

CARLO ANTONI   *From History to Sociology: The Transition in German Historical Thinking* (London, Merlin Press, 1962). First published in 1940 as *Dallo Storicismo alla Sociologia*. Charts the 'decline' of German historical thought into sociology, from a Crocean perspective (see Croce's forward). Detailed discussions of Dilthey, Weber, Troeltsch, Meinecke, Huizinga and Wölfflin.

RAYMOND ARON   *Philosophie critique de l'histoire* (Paris, NRF 11969) Originally published in 1938. Clear and useful analyses of Dilthey, Rickert, Simmel and Weber.

H. A. HODGES   *Wilhelm Dilthey. An Introduction* (London, Routledge, 1944). Includes a number of extracts from Dilthey's writings.
The Philosophy of Wilhelm Dilthey (London, Routledge, 1952). A longer work.

H. STUART HUGHES   *Consciousness and Society. The Reorientation of European Social Thought 1890–1930* (London, Paladin, 1973). First published in 1958. An interesting survey of the reaction against positivism.

RICHARD PALMER   *Hermeneutics* (Evanston, Northwestern University Press, 1969).

H. P. RICKMAN   *Meaning in History. Wilhelm Dilthey's Thoughts on History and Society* (London, George Allen & Unwin, 1961). Extracts from Dilthey's writings with an introduction.
Understanding and the Human Studies (London, Heinemann, 1967). A rather general account of some philosophical issues raised by *Verstehen*.

W. G. RUNCIMAN   *A Critique of Max Weber's Philosophy of Social Science* (Cambridge University Press, 1972).

ALEXANDER von SCHELTING   *Max Weber's Wissenschaftslehre* (Tübingen, Mohr, 1934). An outstanding work on Weber's philosophy of social science; formed the basis of Parson's interpretation of Weber in *The Structure of Social Action*. (See also Parsons's review in *American Sociological Review* 1936.)

KARL-HEINZ SPIELER   *Droysen* (Berlin, Duncker, 1970).

ALFRED STEIN   *Der Begriff des Verstehens bei Dilthey* (Tübingen, Mohr, 1926). First pub. 1913 (in a slightly different form) as *Der Begriff des Geistes bei Dilthey*.

ERNST TROELTSCH   *Der Historismus und seine Probleme, Gesammelte Schriften* Vol. 3 (Tübingen, Mohr, 1923).

JOACHIM WACH   *Das Verstehen, Grundzüge einer Geschichte der hermeneutischen Theorie im neunzehnten Jahrhundert,* 3 vols (Tübingen, Mohr, 1926, 1929, 1933).

RUDOLF WEINGARTNER   *Experience and Culture: The Philosophy of George Simmel* (Wesleyan University Press, 1960).

2a) Writers Influenced by Marxism

MAX ADLER   *Das Rätsel der Gesellschaft. Zur erkenntniskritischen Grundlegung der Sozialwissenschaft* (Vienna, Saturn Verlag, 1936).

LUCIEN GOLDMANN   *The Human Sciences and Philosophy* (London, Jonathan Cape, 1969), first pub. 1952 as *Sciences Humaines et Philosophie.*
Recherches Dialectiques (Paris, Gallimard, 1959).
Marxisme et sciences humaines (Paris, Gallimard, 1970).
'*Introduction aux premiers écrits de G. Lukács*', *Les Temps Modernes* (August 1962).
'The Sociology of Literature', *International Social Science Journal* (1967).

GEORG LUKÁCS   *Soul and Form* (London, Merlin Press, 1974), first pub. 1910 as *Die Seele und die Formen.*
The Theory of the Novel (London, Merlin Press, 1971), first pub. 1920 as *Die Theorie des Romans.*
History and Class Consciousness (London, Merlin Press, 1971), first pub. 1923 as *Geschichte und Klassenbewusstsein.*
Georg Lukács: Schriften zur Literatursoziologie, ed. Peter Ludz (Neuwied, Luchterhand, 1961).

KARL MANNHEIM   *Ideology and Utopia* (London, Routledge, 1936), an expanded version of *Ideologie und Utopie,* first pub. 1929.
Essays on Sociology and Social Psychology, ed. Paul Kecskemeti (London, Routledge, 1953).
Essays on the Sociology of Culture, ed. Ernest Manheim (London, Routledge, 1956).
Essays on the Sociology of Knowledge, ed. Paul Kecskemeti (London, Routledge, 1952).
Karl Mannheim: Wissenssoziologie, ed. Kurt Wolff (Neuwied, Luchterhand, 1964).
From Karl Mannheim, ed. Kurt Wolff (Oxford University Press, 1971).

OTTO NEURATH   *Empiricism and Sociology* (Dordrecht, Reidel, 1973). See in particular the essay on 'Empirical Sociology', first published in 1931.

JEAN-PAUL SARTRE   *Critique de la raison dialectique* (Paris, Gallimard, 1960).

The Problem of Method (London, Methuen, 1963) Trans.
of the prefatory essay in the *Critique*.

2b) Secondary Discussions of These Writers and of the Frankfurt School

MARTIN JAY

*The Dialectical Imagination. A History of the Frankfurt
School and the Institute of Social Research, 1923–1950*
(London, Heinemann, 1973). An outstanding introduc-
tion to this important neo-Marxist movement.

GARETH STEDMAN JONES

'The Marxism of the Early Lukács', *New Left Review*
(1970).

THELMA LAVINE

'Karl Mannheim and Contemporary Functionalism',
Philosophy and Phenomenological Research (1965)
reprinted in G. Remmling (ed.), *Towards the Sociology
of Knowledge* (London, Routledge, 1973).

ISTVAN MÉSZAROS

Lukács' Concept of the Dialectic (London, Merlin
Press, 1972). Includes biographical information about
Lukács, and some illustrations.

ALBRECHT WELLMER

Critical Theory of Society (New York, Herder &
Herder, 1971), first pub. 1969 as *Kritische Gesell-
schaftstheorie und Positivismus*. A difficult but useful
introduction to the 'critical theory' of the Frankfurt
school. See also Martin Jay, *The Dialectical Imagination*.

3) Recent General Works

KARL-OTTO APEL

*Analytic Philosophy of Language and the Geistes-
wissenschaften* (Dordrecht, Reidel, 1967), first pub.
1965 in the *Philosophisches Jahrbuch*. This is an
interesting attempt to show how contemporary analytic
philosophy, though growing out of logical positivism,
has come to share some of the hermeneutic preoccupations of the *Geisteswissenschaft* tradition.

HANS-GEORG GADAMER

Wahrheit und Methode (Tübingen, Mohr, 2nd edn,
1965), first pub. 1960.

JÜRGEN HABERMAS

Zur Logik der Sozialwissenschaften (Frankfurt, Suhrkamp, 1970), first pub. 1967. An outstanding survey of
modern social science and the 'dualism' of the social
and natural sciences.
Knowledge and Human Interests (New York, Beacon
Press, 1971), first pub. 1968 as *Erkenntnis und Interesse*.
A history of positivist thought.

R. HARRÉ and
P. F. SECORD

The Explanation of Social Behaviour. (Oxford, Blackwell,
1972). Argues that social science as practised by, in
particular, Goffman and Garfinkel, is close to the
practice of the natural sciences if these are seen in
'realist' terms.

BARRY HINDESS — *The Use of Official Statistics in Sociology. A Critique of Positivism and Ethnomethodology* (London, Macmillan, 1973). An interesting recent work, written from a standpoint strongly influenced by Louis Althusser, and the French philosopher of science Gaston Bachelard.

LESZEK KOLAKOWSKI — *Positivist Philosophy. From Hume to the Vienna Circle* (Harmondsworth, Penguin, 1972), first pub. 1966 as *Filozofia Pozytywystyczna*. An excellent short introduction to positivism in its many forms.

G. H. VON WRIGHT — *Explanation and Understanding* (London, Routledge, 1971). An interesting attempt by a modern logician to mediate between analytic philosophy and the hermeneutics of the *Geisteswissenschaft* tradition. Von Wright also suggests a possible model of teleological explanation.

Articles

THEODORE ABEL — 'The Operation Called *Verstehen*', *American Journal of Sociology*, Vol. 54 (1948). This influential article should be read critically. It is essentially an attempt to salvage a concept of *Verstehen* acceptable to positivistic social science.

JEFF COULTER — 'Decontextualised Meanings: Current Approaches to *Verstehende* Investigations', *Sociological Review* (1971).

DIANA LEAT — 'Misunderstanding *Verstehen*', *Sociological Review*, (1972).

CHARLES TAYLOR — 'Interpretation and the Sciences of Man', *Review of Metaphysics* (1971).

4) 'Phenomenological' Sociology and Ethnomethodology.

P. BERGER and T. LUCKMANN — *The Social Construction of Reality* (Harmondsworth, Penguin, 1967).

AARON CICOUREL — *Method and Measurement in Sociology* (Glencoe Free Press 1964).

H. P. DREITZEL (ed.) — *Recent Sociology No. 2. Patterns of Communicative Behavior* (New York, Macmillan, 1970).

P. FILMER et al. — *New Directions in Sociological Theory* (London, Collier-Macmillan, 1972). See, in particular, the paper by David Walsh.

H. GARFINKEL — *Studies in Ethnomethodology* (Hemel Hempstead, Prentice-Hall, 1967).

EDO PIVČEVIĆ — *Husserl and Phenomenology* (London, Hutchinson, 1970). 'Can There Be a Phenomenological Sociology?', *Sociology* (1972).

ALFRED SCHUTZ   op. cit. (see section 1(a))

ROY TURNER   *Ethnomethodology* (Harmondsworth, Penguin, 1974). A useful collection of papers.

5) Analytic Philosophy

A. R. LOUCH   *Explanation and Human Action* (Oxford University Press, 1966). Argues 'that observation, description and explanation of human action is only possible by means of moral categories' (p.vii).

ALASDAIR MACINTYRE   'The Idea of a Social Science', *Aristotelian Society*, supplementary volume (1967). Also in A. MacIntyre, *Against the Self-Images of the Age* (London Duckworth, 1971) and in A. Ryan (ed.), *The Philosophy of Social Explanation* (Oxford University Press, 1973).

CHARLES TAYLOR   *The Explanation of Behaviour* (London, Routledge, 1964). Argues that the behaviour of human beings and the higher animals can be explained in teleological terms 'at the most basic level'.
'Explaining Actions', *Inquiry* (1970).

PETER WINCH   *The Idea of a Social Science and its Relation to Philosophy* (London, Routledge, 1958).
'Understanding a Primitive Society', *American Philosophical Quarterly* (1964).

LUDWIG WITTGENSTEIN   *Philosophical Investigations* (Oxford, Blackwell, 1953).

6) Other Works Referred To:

MAX ADLER   *Kausalität und Teleologie im Streite um die Wissenschaft.* In M. A. and R. Hilferding (eds), *Marx-Studien* (Vienna, *Verlag der Wiener Buchhandlung Ignaz Brand* 1904).

HAROLD BERSHADY   *Ideology and Social Knowledge* (Oxford, Blackwell, 1973). An interesting (though somewhat laborious and stylistically appalling) interpretation of the work of Talcott Parsons.

ERNST CASSIRER   *The Logic of the Humanities* (Yale University Press, 1961).

S. COHEN and L. TAYLOR   *Psychological Survival. The Experience of Long-Term Imprisonment* (Harmondsworth, Penguin, 1972).

R. G. COLLINGWOOD   *An Autobiography* (Oxford University Press, 1938).

EMILE DURKHEIM   *Suicide* (London, Routledge, 1952), first pub. 1898.

D. EMMET and A. MACINTYRE (eds)   *Sociological Theory and Philosophical Analysis* (London, Macmillan, 1970).

J. A. FODOR and
J. J. KATZ (eds)
The Structure of Language: Readings in the Philosophy of Language (Hemel Hempstead, Prentice-Hall, 1964).

PATRICK GARDINER (ed.) *Theories of History* (New York, Free Press, 1959).

ANTHONY GIDDENS
Positivism and Sociology (London, Heinemann, 1974).

PETER HAMILTON
Knowledge and Social Structure (London, Routledge, 1974).

KARL JASPERS
General Psychopathology (Manchester University Press, 1962), first pub. 1913 as *Allgemeine Psychopathologie.*

HERBERT MARCUSE
Hegels Ontologie und die Grundlegung einer Theorie der Geschichtlichkeit (Frankfurt, Klostermann, 1968), first pub. 1932.

TULLIO DE MAURO
Ludwig Wittgenstein: His Place in the Development of Semantics (Dordrecht, Reidel, 1967).

TALCOTT PARSONS
The Structure of Social Action (Glencoe, Free Press, 1949), first pub. 1934.

NICOS POULANTZAS
Political Power and Social Classes (London, New Left Books, 1973), first pub. 1968 as *Pouvoir politique et classes sociales de l'etat capitaliste.*

GUNTER REMMLING (ed.) *Towards the Sociology of Knowledge* (London, Routledge, 1973).

W. G. RUNCIMAN
Sociology in Its Place (Cambridge University Press, 1970).

ALAN RYAN
The Philosophy of the Social Sciences (London, Macmillan, 1970).

(ed.)
The Philosophy of Social Explanation (Oxford University Press, 1973).

KAROL SAUERLAND
Diltheys Erlebnisbegriff (Berlin, de Gruyter, 1972).

MAX SCHELER
Die Wissensformen und die Gesellschaft, Vol. 8 (Werke, Bern and Munich, Franke Verlag, 2nd edn, 1960).
The Nature of Sympathy (London, Routledge, 1970), first pub. 1913 as *Phänomenologie der Sympathiegefühle.*

ALFRED SCHMIDT
The Concept of Nature in Marx (London, Merlin Press, 1971), first pub. in 1962 as *Der Begriff der Natur in der Lehre von Marx.*

JOHN SEARLE
Speech Acts. An Essay in the Philosophy of Language (Cambridge University Press, 1969).

E. SPRANGER
Types of Men (Halle, Niemayer, 3rd edn, 1928), first pub. 1922 as *Lebensformen.*

OTTO STAMMER (ed.)
Max Weber and Sociology Today (Oxford, Blackwell, 1971). Conference papers of the 1964 meeting of the German Sociological Association.

P. F. STRAWSON
Individuals (London, Methuen, 1959).
Meaning and Truth (Oxford University Press, 1970).

DANIEL TAYLOR   *Explanation and Meaning* (Cambridge University Press, 1970).

W. L. WALLACE (ed.) *Sociological Theory* (London, Heinemann, 1969)

LUDWIG WITTGENSTEIN *Tractatus Logico-Philosophicus* (London, Kegan Paul, 1923).
                     Remarks on the Foundations of Mathematics (Oxford, Blackwell, 1956).

Index

Abel, Theodore 12, 49, 85, 105n, 117
Action(s) 14, 16, 31–2, 35, 47–8, 50–1, 54, 65–8, 76, 82–6, 88–9, 91, 93–5, 97–8, 100–1, 105; rational 48, 51n; identification of 13–14, 16, 50, 52, 76; theory, frame of reference 67, 86–7; contrasted with behaviour 48, 83, 94
Adler, Max 57–62, 64; concept of *Verstehen* 58–60; and Simmel 59–61
Adorno, Theodor 62
'Alien' beliefs, cultures, societies 52, 85, 96, 106–9
Analytic philosophy 7, 12, 26, 43n, 50, 82, 94, 108, 116–18; and *verstehende* sociology 94, 108 (*See* Linguistic analysis, philosophy)
Anthropology 52, 97, 108–9; structural 66–7
Antoni, Carlo 12n, 114
Apel, Karl-Otto 7, 13n, 94n, 116
Aron, Raymond 25n, 44, 46–7, 52n, 53–4, 114
Ast, Friedrich, 19, 20

Behaviour 13–14, 28, 41, 47–9, 51, 54, 63, 68, 83, 89, 94–5, 97, 99; communicative 93; maxim 49, 85
Behaviourism 84–6, 94, 109
Berger, Peter 106, 117
Bergson, Henri 25n
Berlin, Isaiah 25n
Bershady, Harold 87n, 88n, 90, 118
Bismarck 28–9
Boeckh, August 20

Buckle, H. T. 21
Budapest 74

Caesar 28n, 92
Causation 50, 52, 59, 76–7, 105
Cause 32, 42, 50n, 59, 63, 86, 94, 96
Causal generalisation(s) 29, 36, 41, 50; hypotheses 38, 49; imputation 42n; regularities 12, 27–8; verification 53 (*See* Explanation, causal)
Chomsky, Noam 82–3n, 84
Cicourel, Aaron 86, 92–3, 106, 109, 117
Cohen, S. and Taylor, L. 108, 118
Collingwood, R. G. 12, 118
Commodity form 68, 70
Communication 83, 91, 94, 98, 101, 104–5; distorted 62, 102
Communicative competence 101
Comte, Auguste 11, 24, 39
Critical Theory 100, 107 (*See* Frankfurt School)
Croce, Benedetto 12
Cultural objects, phenomena, products 15, 26, 30, 32, 41, 56, 71, 74–7, 80; sciences 38, 41, 77; organisations 33

Deutung (*See* Interpretation)
Dilthey, Wilhelm 7, 20, 23–38, 56–7, 62–3, 71, 83, 98, 103–5, 113–14; and *Verstehen* 12, 24, 26–36, 62; and functionalism 33; and *Lebensphilosophie* 62–3; and psychology 26–30, 34; and sociology 29; and Rickert 36, 40–1, 43; and Simmel 36, 44–5; and Weber 36, 46; and Winch 98

126 *Index*

GLASGOW
UNIVERSITY
LIBRARY